The Good, The Bad & The Hooligan

Tales from the Glen

A compilation of
'Josine's Garden Blog'
as read in the
Stirling Health Food Store
monthly newsletter

From Josine

Josine Atsma

The Good, The Bad & The Hooligan

Tales from the Glen

A compilation of
'Josine's Garden Blog'

as read in the
Stirling Health Food Store
monthly newsletter

A Small Steps Publication

A Small Steps Publication
www.smallstepsonline.net

First published 2019

British Library Cataloguing in Publication Data
A catalogue record for this book is available from the British Library.

ISBN: 978-1-9162658-1-3

Layout by Stuart Ainslie

Printed and bound in the UK

This book is dedicated to my parents
Paul and Rina
who introduced me to home growing.

CONTENTS

MISCELLANY

ACKNOWLEDGEMENTS

I'd firstly like to thank my husband, JP for his continued support, encouragement, hard work and - of course - for building all those wonderful structures in the garden practically single handedly!

Thanks also must go to my neighbours for turning a blind eye to the havoc my chickens cause on their side of the fence; all the wwoofers who have toiled so tirelessly over the years in the garden; the hens - especially the ill tempered, potty mouthed 'The Hooligan' - for giving me so much material to write about; and a heartfelt thank you to the customers who frequent our humble little store and to those who go to the trouble of reading the Stirling Health Food Store newsletter every month and for their kind comments.

A special thank you to Stuart Ainslie for helping put this book together and for his help in editing the newsletter - adding in the occasional naff joke, silly pun and the odd Star Wars reference.

But most of all I'm grateful for the wonder, beauty and splendour of 'Mother Nature'. 'Veel dank' for providing me with so much inspiration and for enriching the world we live in!

FOREWORD

by Leigh Biagi

As a regular customer of the Stirling Health Food Store, a passionate gardener, a committed environmentalist and a keen reader of 'Josine's Garden and Chicken Blog' I am delighted that Josine has decided to compile her hugely entertaining writings in a book; 'The Good, the Bad and The Hooligan'.

I enjoy reading about other people's adventures in gardening almost as much as I enjoy gardening myself, and through Josine's descriptions in her blog of her harvest triumphs and disasters over the years, I have felt reassured that I am not the only one whose runner beans have disappointed or kale has been eaten by snails, slugs, birds or even chickens. I share her passion for producing organic, home-grown veg, and I share her desire to create a productive garden which works in synergy with nature and provides a much-needed haven for wildlife. The one area where our passions diverge is Josine's love of chickens; but that hasn't stopped me enjoying tales of her wayward brood, particularly the aptly named 'The Hooligan'.

In recent years I have been very grateful for Josine's support of my project 'On the Verge' which encourages community groups and individuals to sow wildflower areas wherever they can. She has promoted the work of 'On the Verge' in the shop, given out free wildflower seeds on our behalf and even donated proceeds from the carrier bag fund to our organisation. I look forward to continuing to work with Josine into the future to encourage others to sow and grow - and I look forward to more blogs!

Leigh Biagi
Chair 'On the Verge'
October 2019

INTRODUCTION

At various times in my life I've wanted to be either: a surgeon; a professional organic farmer; a writer or a film editor. Some of these vocations I considered more seriously than others.

Now all grown up and in my 40's I am neither of these. Yet, I do all to some degree or other. I advise people on health issues; I grow my own food organically; I've also had a brush with film and TV and I write!

In this book you will be taken on a journey through the different seasons of the year, so be prepared for lots of snow; strong winds; torrential rain and long, dry sunny spells. From failures in the garden to successfully growing monster-sized vegetables you will read about the challenges we've faced; the struggles we've had. The little battles we've won and lost.

The first newsletter came out way back in June 2012. Even harder to believe is that the first couple of issues didn't even have a garden blog! As I like blethering about my garden to anyone who wants to listen and didn't want to distract customers shopping in my store *too* much, my 'Garden Blog' was born. So in August 2012 'Josine's Garden Blog' first appeared. Fast forward 7 years, a whopping 85 newsletters and almost 300 subscribers later and here we are, a compilation of the garden blogs with a sprinkling of tips on eco-living; how to grow-your-own fruit and veg; and some stories seeing the light of day for the very first time.

Looking back, the first blogs were very basic and bare, just like the garden itself. It began to grow and bloom over time as I myself grew more confident in writing about my garden and other subjects.

Weather has always been a big part of my blogs, both because I am slightly obsessed with the weather (what gardener isn't?), but also because it hugely influences what grows and what doesn't. The strong winds and heavy snowfall we get up here in Glendevon certainly doesn't make things easy and I often envy my parents who grow their own vegetables in the Netherlands and who are always months ahead of us.

When our first five chickens arrived in October 2013 one of them suddenly emerged as the star of my blog. This plucky, 'fowl' mouthed hen (affectionately known as 'The Hooligan') soon became Stirling's most famous chicken. We shared many adventures together her and I, which in turn gave me plenty to write about. She even appeared with me and my husband on the small screen, when our garden featured in an episode of the BBC's 'The Beechgrove Garden' in May 2015. The popularity of the chickens meant I had to change the name of my blog to accommodate them, renaming it 'Josine's Garden & Chicken Blog'.

During late 2017 and early 2018 I started doing a bit of work as an 'extra' for TV and film (something which had always been high up on my bucket list) and I began including these experiences in my blog too. With appearances in Scotland's one and only home grown soap 'River City', several TV dramas and the odd feature film, it all made for extra footage, er, extra stories for the newsletter.

I don't have a background in botany or farming, everything I have learned comes from books I've read and experiences I've had. I am not a preacher, nor an eco-warrior. All I want to do is share my stories, my struggles and my successes and perhaps inspire someone, somewhere, to grow at least some of their own food or go that bit further and transform their garden into a wildlife haven.

Over the years the garden has grown, gone from strength to strength. Come to life. Unrecognisable from that bare, uninspired piece of land we inherited when we moved to Glendevon. It is totally transformed and so has my 'blog'.

And I hope you feel inspired to sow a seed or two, after all, seeds are included with this book!

So join me in planting a seed. Together we will watch it grow.

Josine Atsma
October 2019

2012

The Full Minty

It's hard to believe now, back when I started the Stirling Health Food Store Newsletter in June 2012, there was no sign of a blog at all. Just a few items of shop news and a list of products on special offer. It wasn't until a few months later that my first '**Garden Blog**' appeared. After that, there was no looking back!

August

By now you probably all know I like talking about my garden, so instead of boring you in the shop with my chatter I thought I'd write down my gardening news and include it in this month's newsletter. Making it a regular monthly feature.

My husband and I live in the tiny village of Glendevon, about 20 miles from Stirling, in between the Ochils. It is a very exposed area with plenty of midges, cold nights (just recorded 4°C in July) and strong winds. Growing vegetables is not always an easy thing to do, but then again I quite enjoy a bit of a challenge!

Trying to be self-sufficient in vegetables most of the year, we grow all the usual suspects: potatoes, onions, carrots, cabbages and so forth.

However with all the cold and wet weather we've had, I doubt it if we will get any French beans or carrots because they both look very poorly.

But I have lifted the first potatoes, a variety called 'Orla' and they are quite nice and I also had a meagre crop of mangetout.

September

I always say: "If Monty Don has difficulties growing vegetables, then I'll be lucky if I can grow anything at all!"

I think we all agree that it has been pretty cold and wet this summer, so growing fruit and vegetables hasn't been the easiest task. However there were some success stories: the currants and gooseberries have been growing well, so I made lots of jam (around 40 jars at the last count!) and I also have a gooseberry wine on the go.

Actually, gooseberry wine (or 'The Goose, the Berry and the Ugly' as we like to call it) is a very tasty white wine and almost indistinguishable from a good hock.

Two things that never fail are my swedes and turnips. I grow 'Purple Top Milan' swedes and they always perform well, no matter what the weather throws at them.

I have now started digging up my early main crop potatoes, a variety known as 'Remarka', which has yielded some really nice potatoes. Just as well I am fond of neeps and tatties!

The rest of the veg is just slow, slow, slow. The cabbage heads have just started forming; the sprouts are only about one foot high and the (runner) beans are just beginning to flower.

So, fingers crossed we will get an Indian Summer!*

October

Dear, oh dear... more strong winds! Living in the hills is nice, but we're very exposed to westerly winds this high up (240m/787ft), so growing runner beans can be a challenge. If the early frost doesn't kill them, the wind will finish them off!

This year I've only harvested one pathetic looking runner bean....

There is good news too though. This year I grew my courgettes under a lightweight poly tunnel (which needless to say, blew away in the high winds!) BUT my courgettes survived the winds and now that they are back under their cosy poly tunnel again - they've started to grow!

As you all know there aren't many elderberries this year, so I can't make elderberry wine from the fresh fruits and I will have to make do with dried elderberries instead. That's a nice job to do on a wet and windy day (of which there have been quite a few recently!). There are, however, advantages to living in a windy area: the cabbage butterfly just gets blown passed the cabbages;

* *Needless to say we didn't!*

19

we don't have many slugs either and the carrot fly faces the same problem as the butterflies - too windy to land!

It won't be long now before all I'll have to tell you about the garden is that we've had snow, snow and more snow...

On the evening of Monday 15th October, at a rather glitzy award ceremony in Glasgow, Josine and staff from the Stirling Health Food Store were presented with the award for '**Best Scottish Independent Retailer Health & Lifestyle 2012**'! Yaayyyy! The trophy is still proudly displayed in the shop for all to see.

November

We've had a few nice days, warm enough to sit in the sun even; enjoy a game of badminton in the garden and a glass of home made beer. But winter is fast approaching, so that means time to get the garden ready.

I have just planted out my spring cabbages (a variety called 'Offenham'). They look okay now, but whether I'll be eating cabbage in late spring depends on how bad a winter we get!

I have also picked all of my tomatoes. They were still green but if they show even the slightest sign of ripening, then you can wrap them in a tea towel and store them in a warm place (in my case the cupboard where the boiler is kept). After a week or 10 days they should have all ripened - at least mine did anyway!

Actually, I had a much bigger crop of tomatoes this year than

I had last year. Which is strange, considering how cold and wet the summer has been.

I have checked my carrots (a variety called 'Autumn King') and although they are small, they don't show any sign of carrot fly, which is good news at least... I suspect my husband and I will be fighting over the last carrot as usual, because home grown carrots taste so delicious!

From December of this year a **'Did You Know...'** section was added to the newsletter, placed just beneath my 'Garden Blog'.

This fun little addition proved very popular with readers.

Several of these interesting little facts can be found scattered throughout the pages of this book.

December

Well... what can I say?

Of course I haven't been doing much in the garden at this time of year. Although I did plant an oak tree yesterday. We've only got a rowan tree and the fruit trees in our garden, so I thought it might be a good idea to plant an oak. And in Glendevon we have an enclave of red squirrels, so they will benefit from it too!

When it's too cold to be outside all you can do is flick through garden magazines and dream about the new vegetables you are going to plant in the Spring. I might try and find purple carrots to grow next year, but so far I haven't found ones which are purple on the inside too. So, if any of you know where to lay your hands on these...

My husband has been braver than me and planted a completely new beech hedge to shelter the vegetable plot from strong easterly winds. On the west side we are growing a native hedge, consisting of hawthorn, blackthorn and rosehips, again good for wildlife (and also for making wine and sloe gin, of course!).

2013

E.B.: The Extra Berrestrial

January

This year I am going to carry out an experiment. I'm going to try my hand at 'biodynamic' gardening. Biodynamic gardening is one step up from organic gardening in the sense that you also take into account lunar and planetary cycles. Because I'm no astronomer, I need a biodynamic calendar to keep me right - to tell me what to do and when to do it. Luckily, this comes in the form of a book. You can have 'leaf days' (i.e. cabbages and lettuces), 'flower days', 'fruit days' (i.e. courgettes and tomatoes) or 'no-no days' which means you can't do very much at all really.

I haven't made my mind up yet if biodynamic gardening really produces healthier plants, but if the moon can cause whole oceans to rise and fall, it makes sense that the moon could also influence the sap in plants.

That's really why I'm doing this experiment: I'll sow some seeds according to the biodynamic calendar and other seeds randomly and just see what happens.

Come September I hope to let you know how the vegetables have fared. So, watch this space!

February

'Let it snow, let it snow, let it snow!'

Sorry, the present climate might have been my fault for singing this all January...

We've certainly had more snow than I could have imagined. In Glendevon about 40cm (16 inches) of snow fell in just four days, completely covering the raised vegetable beds where we've been growing our cabbages. I have to admit when my husband and I had to abandon our car at the bottom of the hill we live on, it was quite romantic struggling through the snow late at night with just a torch beam to light our way!

Anyway that's it all melted now, although we might get some more later in the month, who knows?

Slowly I have started sowing vegetables: the chillies, tomatoes and aubergines are all snug and warm in the house, sitting on the windowsill. The first lot I have sown (according to the moon) and later I will sow the exact same seeds when it's a 'no-no day'.

For those who missed the last newsletter, I'm doing an experiment in 'biodynamic' gardening, which has specific guidelines for what to sow and just as importantly, when to sow.

We get lots of bubble wrap with some of our shop deliveries - so

I repurpose it to insulate the greenhouse, cold frames and plant pots. I don't like throwing anything away!

March

I can hardly believe it. Spring already!

Erm... what happened to February exactly? It started off way too cold to do anything in the garden, but in the last week or so the weather has improved and I finally enjoyed a pleasant afternoon digging some vegetable beds and weeding, followed by feeding and mulching the fruit trees. So, that's one job out of the way at least. Or four to be exact.

In March I've got a week off and will hopefully be able to do more in the garden. My husband wants to build me a poly tunnel for not so hardy veg. Only slight problem is... where he wants to build it there is already a bed full of strawberries. So, we now need to create a new bed for the strawberries and since I make my own jam (strawberry amongst others), it's going to have to be a BIG bed. A 'king size' one perhaps?

Fingers crossed it will be nice and dry and not pouring with rain the week I'm off, as so often happens...

In my biodynamic experiment the aubergines I've sowed under the most preferable circumstances ('yes-yes fruit day') have germinated well, but the aubergines I've sowed on a 'no-no day' have also germinated very well, even without the greenhouse lid! But its way too early to say whether biodynamic creates stronger plants or not. I'll keep you posted on the aubergines (which hopefully will have a new poly tunnel to grow in soon).

April

What on earth is going on?!

Last newsletter I was chatting about how I was looking forward to getting started in the garden soon and now *this*!

More snow. And lots of it! It's hard to tell exactly how much snow has fallen (at a rough guess about 20 inches) but the snow drifts were much higher this time - up to my waist - high enough to bury my fruit bushes. I've also got a honey berry bush which is native to Siberia, which probably means it loves this weather! I hope so! I was planning to plant my early potatoes next week, but I think I might just wait a wee bit longer and see what happens...

To cheer myself up I bought some compost and sowed some cabbages, Brussels sprouts and the appropriately named 'winter savoury'. Winter savoury is an herb which you can use to bring out the flavour in beans - in Dutch it goes by the name of (rather unsurprisingly) 'bean herb'!

There is not much to tell about my biodynamic gardening experiment - except everything has more or less stopped growing.

Surely it will get warmer some day... soon?

May

Temperatures have risen, ever so slightly - warm enough for the first swallow to arrive! It means I've been out into the garden planting my potatoes (a few weeks too late, but never mind). I also planted some onion sets and sowed nasturtiums in between the 'kapucijners' beans, which (as you may have already guessed) are a Dutch variety of bean which can withstand temperatures as low as -5°C! Besides my trial in biodynamic gardening, I'll also experiment with 'permaculture'. Permaculture involves planting several different species of plants close to one another. For example, nasturtiums grown in between bean plants will attract aphids away from your beans (to the nasturtiums) and it will also attract pollinators. What I wonder is this... if you plant everything close together does that mean it will be a bit warmer between the plants?!

We'll soon find out!

Before I moved to Scotland I did a lot of volunteering on organic farms, crofts and smallholdings all over Scotland. This was such a great experience that my husband and I decided we wanted to offer others that same experience. Although we are nowhere near as big as a farm or a smallholding, we can still do with a helping hand in our garden. There is an organisation called WWOOF which brings volunteers and hosts together.

In exchange for free lodgings - a warm bed and some good grub - the volunteers (or 'wwoofers' as they are known) work several hours a day on your farm (or in our case garden!). We've already had a lot of interest from people all over the world: America, France and Italy. It is very exciting to have complete strangers stay in your home and I'm confident it will work out well - after all we've been there ourselves and had some great experiences! Frankly, one or two of those experiences weren't that great... but they were experiences all the same and I wouldn't change them for anything!

If you are interested in becoming a host or volunteer you can find their details on page 189 of this book.

June

I'll be in Switzerland for a few days this month checking out the herb gardens of A. Vogel and learning how they make their herbal tinctures. But before that there are also lots of things to do now in my own garden...

Most of the vegetables and flowers have been sowed by now and, so far so good as most of them are coming up and seem to be growing well. Although I still have had no luck with beetroot! What is it with beetroot? Beets me... I've been trying to grow it for several years now and so far I haven't been able to harvest one decent sized beetroot! It's very frustrating - I have no idea what I'm doing wrong. Also the runner beans didn't like being transplanted, so I decided to sow some extra beans at the same time just in case. Hopefully they should come up.

My husband (and his father, who is visiting from the Netherlands) will be busy the next few weeks building a 6m x 3m greenhouse from scratch. We are in such an exposed location that it needs to be extra sturdy. My hubby is a very clever chap so I've no doubt that the finished structure will be very impressive indeed.

From the first day we registered as WWOOF hosts, we've had lots of requests from volunteers to help us. From America to Taiwan and from Germany to Spain - we've had replies from all over the globe. So many that we've unfortunately had to turn quite a few down. A German girl will be coming over to help out in July and August and then two Italian girls will join us at the end of August. It's going to be an exciting time - not only for them but for us, too!

July

Wow! Plants have definitely been growing! I've picked my first new potatoes, the first tomatoes are beginning to show and the weeds, well, they are growing too! In those four days I was away in Switzerland, the runner beans almost burst through the poly tunnel and the Dutch kapucijners are flowering like crazy.

Luckily for me, I'll welcome our very first wwoofer on Monday (Tatjana from Germany) and hopefully we'll get stuck into those weeds, get the bean poles erected and have time left over to make some elderflower champagne.

It will be hard work but very exciting too!

Not so good news on the gooseberry front, though: a terrible attack of sawfly stripped almost all the leaves off one of my gooseberry bushes. I'm not sure if the fruit will keep growing now - I suppose there is not much I can do, so no point worrying about it. Waste of energy!

I promised to share some tips and tricks I learned at the A. Vogel Museum in Switzerland, so here they are: 'Scratch' the soil everyday to keep the weeds away! Basically, it means that if you hoe or scratch the soil everyday for around 5 minutes, the weeds can't keep hold and if you do this first thing in the morning before work, you'll also start the day with some low-key yoga!

They also used upside down terracotta pots with straw in them to attract beneficial insects (like earwigs) which in turn eat red spider mite.

And they practised 'permaculture', which is something that interests me greatly. It means that you grow vegetables next to flowering plants with no need to really stick to a schedule. I'm trying that in some of my beds at the moment, just to see the difference if any - as usual, I'll keep you posted on how I get on in future blogs...

August

Wow and double Wow! What amazing weather we've had lately! The fruit and vegetables are doing so much better than last year. Take my French beans for instance, last year they never grew beyond the size they were when I planted them, but this year they are already reaching the top of their poles. The strawberry bed is proving to be a success too, so far I've picked well over 7kg (15.5lbs) of strawberries! That's a lot of jam and, of course, the odd bottle of strawberry wine or two! The runner beans are flowering nicely - I've got the variety 'Moonlight' which are supposed to do well in poor weather conditions. (I needn't worry too much about that this year!). The first runner beans are showing, but unfortunately, the dry weather has also meant that my sweet peas have shrivelled up after producing just a few flowers. Ah well - can't win 'em all, I suppose!

And... at last! Our greenhouse is finished, thanks to my husband and our wwoofer from Germany! It surprised me just how much more you can get done with an extra pair of helping hands. I'm also curious to see what difference there will be between the squashes growing inside the greenhouse and the ones growing outside. Thyme, sorry, time will tell!

September

Wow! Wow and triple Wow! What a difference the better weather has made to my vegetables! Do you remember that last year I only had one miserable, pathetic looking runner bean? Well, this year we've already had enough for a meal or two, with some left over to give away to our neighbours! And there are still lots more small beans and flowers.

Have you also noticed that there are more bumblebees around this year? Or maybe it's just because I sowed some dahlia, sunflower and calendula seeds in our garden and the bees love the full grown flowers? One sunflower even had four drowsy, drunk looking bumblebees on it, all at the same time!

And what a great help the wwoofers have been! As I mentioned last time the greenhouse is finished; all the vegetables beds have been weeded and hopefully in September we will be welcoming 5 rescue hens into our newly built chicken house! Rescue hens are ex-battery hens which no longer lay eggs in any great numbers. They would otherwise be killed because of this. I would like them to see and feel the sun (or rain!) and be able to run around freely for the rest of their days, before passing away from natural causes.

If you're also interested in 'saving' some chickens, details of the British Hen Welfare Trust can be found on page 189 of this book.

> With the arrival of our 5 rescue hens there is suddenly so much more to write about! From October 2013 onwards, 'Josine's Garden Blog' expands and now becomes 'Josine's Garden and **Chicken** Blog'!
>
> It's not long before they become the real stars of the show - one cranky, potty mouthed chicken in particular...

October

Hello and welcome to our new, free range life, chickens!

Yes, my husband and our American wwoofer collected 5 rescue hens last Saturday afternoon and the very next morning ALL of them had laid an egg (the hens that is, not my husband nor our wwoofer!). A very nice little gift from them.

We gave the chickens a few drops of 'Emergency Pet Essence', a herbal remedy from A. Vogel, which has apparently helped them to settle in. They are making themselves at home, trying out scratching; trying to eat a worm (very funny to watch, but not much fun for the worm I'm guessing); trying to eat apples and generally behaving like chickens. Clucking and squawking and such like...

Our neighbours also have two chickens which we call the 'Daleks', since they 'exterminate' everything in sight and won't rest until the entire universe is in their evil clutches. Well, maybe not that last part, but who knows for sure? Anyhow, we now have the 'Ginger Ninjas' to thwart their evil plans! Haa-Yaa! (That's the sound of a karate chop, by the way!)

We have also been making lots of wine this month: gooseberry, strawberry, autumn oak leaf, rowanberry and elderflower. Now we are waiting for the elderberries to ripen so we can make elderberry wine and elderberry/bramble wine, which tastes quite delicious.

The runner beans continue to surpass my expectations - if you remember I only had one measly, miserable looking runner bean last year.

This year we're heading towards 2kg! Everything has performed so much better, apart from the potatoes which we didn't water in the dry spell (in Holland you don't water your potatoes). So they turned out pretty small which is disappointing. Never mind, though, because everything else has performed exceedingly well!

November

Last month we welcomed our last wwoofer of the year, a 21 year old girl from France whose understanding of English wasn't that great (or maybe she has a problem understanding our mix of Dutch/Scottish accents!) but that makes it all the more challenging.

October was the month for preserve and wine making. We made hedgerow jelly this time round, a rather strong autumn oak leaf wine (18%! Phew...) and we also started making our own sauerkraut.

Sauerkraut is fermented cabbage, which means that all you add to finely sliced white cabbage is salt and juniper berries for flavouring (although this isn't essential), then all you need to do is 'bash' it (technical term - using a flat hammer or equivalent kitchen utensil) until the water has been released (very good exercise) and leave it in a warm place to ferment. The fermentation process is what makes it sour, so real sauerkraut doesn't contain any vinegar! It is also very healthy, containing a lot of vitamin C and digestive enzymes, which in turn can aid a healthy digestion.

Turn to page 183 for my recipe for making authentic **sauerkraut**.

The chickens are still settling in quite nicely. Some weeks ago they got their first taste of freedom and were allowed to roam completely free in our (and our neighbours') garden. We figured they were able to find their own way back to the coop at night and 4 out of 5 of them did. Unfortunately one of them is not such a clever lass... She has a habit of going 'walkabout' and has already managed to get herself lost twice! One night she came back long after the rest were perched safe and sound inside their coop and had a rather displeased look on her face when she found it was shut. Then a week later she stayed out the whole night. My husband thought it must've ended up as a fox's main course, but I refused to give up hope and sure enough the next night, there she was, trying to remember how to get in. We now call her 'McLucky', because she had been very lucky that night, that's for sure!

Now, chickens don't normally wear jumpers but we had some small woollen pullovers knitted and tried them out on the chickens - to keep them warm when the weather gets very, very cold and when they are moulting and lose their feathers. Needless to say they weren't very impressed and prefer to go 'au naturel'!

December

These chickens of mine... I'm seriously thinking of sending them back. Why? Because they're bonkers, that's why! (I won't though, I love 'em too much!)

They now have collectively decided that I am their mother, food provider and top hen all rolled into one. Now they insist on following me everywhere I go.

As soon as I step out of the back door they come running up to me and won't leave my side until I close the door on them when I go back inside. Having them cling to me all the time makes planting tulips quite challenging... Next Spring I really need to think of a way of keeping them out of the vegetable garden. I might actually build a hatch for them to go into the surrounding fields, so I can lock them out of our garden until I've finished what I'm doing. That's something to think about next year, though, right now they are eating all the bugs and insects I don't want near my plants and that's a good thing! Unless you happen to be one of those bugs or insects that is.

Sadly my trial of storing turnips has failed. I read somewhere that you can store turnips by putting them in a box of sand and keep them in a cold, dry place. But when I decided to make neeps and tatties the other day, I found them all mouldy and hollow on the inside. I'm not sure where I've gone wrong. You live and learn, I suppose.

Anyway, I have managed to make lots of chutney, piccalilli and jam; dried some herbs and beans and made some wine so my larder is pretty full!

I should be okay for the coming winter...

2014

Straw Wars: The Berry Strikes Back

January

With the shortest day out of the way it's time to plan ahead and think about what to sow this spring. I'm sure I'm not the only one frustrated that I can't start sowing just yet. But patience is key if you don't want your vegetables to perish in the cold.

With the brand new big greenhouse my husband built (with the help of his dad and wwoofers) I now have plenty of space to grow lots of tomatoes and cucumbers. But I'm also planning to grow one or two pumpkins this year as well as courgettes, aubergines, chillies and gherkins. The pumpkins are easy to store; the courgettes in case the weather fails; my husband will make sweet & sour chilli sauce from the chillies - and the gherkins, well, I'll pickle those!

Our hens are still doing great, laying plenty of eggs. I don't know why some say chickens don't lay eggs in winter time?! Ours must be very happy and content, that's all I can say...

I'm not sure the chickens had any idea what snow was until they were almost completely covered in the stuff! They still follow us around (*sigh!*) and when we had to call out a plumber over Christmas, he complained the chickens were trying to steal his tools! I had to laugh!

February

My chickens sure bring a smile to my face. We had a nice covering of snow the other day but when I went to let the hens out, they weren't too keen on coming out of their coup! They just stayed in their run looking at each other as if to say: "What on earth has happened to our grass?? Yesterday it was green and prickly and now it's turned white and soft and cold!"

I had to call on them repeatedly and scatter some sunflower seeds for them so that they would venture out (which they did... eventually!).

When they finally got used to the snow, they didn't seem to mind it at all. In fact, I'd go as far as saying they enjoyed themselves! But it was soon back to business - following me around the garden... again!

Those hens of mine are becoming quite the celebrities too; they might need to start their own fan club soon! People in the United States have been reading about them and the British Hen Welfare Trust has posted pictures of them on their website! Next month, they might even make an appearance in the 'Your Chickens'

Magazine. It turned out my picture was chosen as the readers' winning photo for the April 2014 issue of the magazine.

As for growing vegetables, all my new seeds have come in. The fridge is full of seed potatoes and onion sets. I like to keep the potatoes in the fridge until it's time to start chitting them, which will probably be around March time.

But I'm also trying something a bit different - growing mushrooms on a log. First I need to find a suitable log (one that's not too old) - there is one near the river close to us, but it's been too wet and slippery to pull it out. Hopefully when the weather improves, I'll be able to drill some holes in the log, put the mushroom dowels in and seal it with wax. Then after only 2 years (!) I'll be able to harvest my very own mushrooms. Well, that's the plan anyway... I'll let you know how I got on in a couple of years. Unless I forget.

> **Did you know...**
> ... every year around 21st March and 21st September the sun passes the equator, resulting in equal lengths of day and night all over the world? This is known as the **Spring** or **Autumnal Equinox**.

March

Those cheeky wee devils (aka the chickens) are bullying our cat and stealing his prey!

Did you know chickens eat mice as well? Nope, me neither...

until I saw them chasing the cat away and fighting over his (dead) mouse. According to one of my books, chickens sometimes eat larger animals if one is unlucky (or stupid) enough to venture into the hen house. Poor mice, not only do they need to keep one eye open for the cat, but they now have to keep the other eye open for the chickens, too.

Another couple of our chooks have been running away too, preferring the company of the sheep in the field next to us rather than their own kind. Every night we have to double check they're not hanging out with their woolly best pals on the wrong side of the fence. We don't want to give the foxes in the neighbourhood any ideas!

Because of the mild winter we've had so far, a lot of plants have started to come up again. The garlic I planted last November is already 15cm (6") high.

When my husband and I moved to this house, there was only one big rowan tree in our back garden, but a few weeks ago we planted two more trees, a hawthorn and a birch. The garden immediately took on the appearance of a garden, rather than just a plain looking, boring old field. And fifteen minutes after planting the hawthorn, a bird perched on a branch!

Also... the wwoofers are flooding in! We are nearly fully booked for the coming year. We'll be getting Spanish, American, Austrian and Dutch (!) wwoofers this year - and it's only February! Some wwoofers are really well organised, that's all I can say.

As we grow our own vegetables and make our own wine, bread, beer, sauerkraut etc. we can do with an extra pair of hands about the place and that's where the wwoofers come in handy! This is our second year of being wwoof hosts and let's hope it will be as big a success as it was last year!

April

My husband and I have been working on a demo-video about living a self-sufficient life in Scotland, which we intend to send to several Dutch television channels.

I don't trust my English enough to send it to the BBC just yet.

Anyway, we were filming inside our greenhouse and as usual the chickens were misbehaving. They are not allowed in there as a rule, but when they heard me talking, one of them flew straight into the window to try and get a better look! Another found a way of peering in to see what the fuss was all about and more importantly to see if there were any worms involved. Sorry to disappoint them, but there weren't!

They needn't worry though, I'm sure they'll get to make a cameo appearance in the video!

With Easter in mind; two of our hens have now decided to lay their eggs any old place they like! So every day we need to search the garden for any 'missing' eggs. Luckily one of the hens lays her eggs - more times than not - in our wood basket, so that's not too hard to find, but the other one is proving a little bit trickier. A proper, real-life Easter egg-hunt!

Now is the time to get everything ready in the garden. The

windowsill is full of seedlings, the greenhouse is starting to fill up with tiny plants and there are still pumpkins and other 'warmer' vegetables to sow.

The greenhouse gets really warm in the sun, but unfortunately one night in late March we had a temperature of -5°C, which killed a handful of my tomato plants. I still have 38 plants left, which should be enough to fill the entire greenhouse and beyond...

We've also had our first greens fresh from the garden; sorrel and endive (grown in the greenhouse). I'm trying to force rhubarb, but I might have been a bit late with that, because the other rhubarb I planted is also starting to come up again. Ah well, if nothing else, we're not going to be short of rhubarb this year...

May

Wow... a lot has happened in the past few weeks!

In the first week of April one of our hens went AWOL. It was the 'runaway' one, the one who has the habit of running to the neighbours' house and only comes back home when it's time to sleep. Charming. Well, one night she was nowhere to be seen. Nor the next night, nor the next again. This went on for more than a week. Naturally, we thought she had gone for good - caught by a fox or something. Until our neighbour came to our door and told us he had found the hen sitting on a clutch of 16 eggs! She had been feeling particularly broody for some time and had made herself a nice little nest somewhere in the neighbouring field. She's been incredibly lucky a fox didn't find her! So, now we're back to having a full compliment of 5 chickens. A happy (h)ending after all!

A little after that, a (very keen) wwoofer phoned to ask if he could come over that very same day! We could always do with a little bit of extra help, so we agreed. Only to be told two days later that he couldn't cope with the isolation and wanted to leave again! We're not *that* isolated are we? Okay, so we don't have any mobile phone reception, no freeview, a paltry broadband speed of only 70Kb and the nearest public transport is 5 miles away. But apart from that... Anyway, he did work hard, building a saw horse and planting out around 100 onions. Not bad for the brief time he was with us.

So, now all 400 onions (made a mistake ordering them, oops!) have been planted. I haven't got much else in the vegetable plot yet, all other vegetables are sitting nice and warm inside our cosy little greenhouse.

However we've decided to transform our back garden into a 'five senses garden'. Our back garden is just one big field of grass at the moment and the plan is to dig out six borders: five representing our five senses (smell, taste, touch, sight and hearing) and a bed for more 'medicinal' plants.

Believe me, this is going to be a pretty big project! Luckily we've got our first wwoofer coming soon. My husband has got a new 'mega' project: the 'hearing' border. This will consist of a pond with some reeds and plants (which I'll choose a little later). Well, okay, I might help him with some of the digging too...

I'll keep you up-to-date on our progress!

June

I feel as though I should write more often about these hens of mine. They have so many fun adventures! One night when my husband and I came home we found four chickens waiting for us, but there was no sign of the fifth one. I thought I heard a clucking sound coming from over by the car, but my husband was adamant he couldn't see anything, even checking underneath it just to make sure. The stupid thing had managed to get stuck under the 'poo bucket' we use to clean the hen house with every morning! How she got there is anybody's guess but she probably jumped on the edge and tipped it over onto herself. Poor thing! We don't know for sure how long she had been there, but she certainly looked a bit dazed when we rescued her. Mind you, sometimes they can be quite clever - perhaps she was using the bucket to shelter from the rain (or playing a game of hide and seek, who knows?).

The blossom is looking good this year. All the fruit trees are covered in it and luckily we haven't had any late frost. Now we have to wait and see if the summer will be warm enough to allow the fruit to ripen.

The wwoofing season has also started! We had an American girl staying in May and a Dutch guy is due to pay us a visit in July. We've been making parsley wine and sweet cicely wine; planted lots of tomatoes in the greenhouse and have sowed our wildflower bed.

The American wwoofer was really impressed by how many weeds are actually edible: ground elder, comfrey, nettle, sorrel and dock were all on the menu while she stayed with us. She now wants to grow things herself. It won't be easy though, she grew up in the outskirts of Las Vegas, which is basically a desert - just an ever-so-slightly different climate from Scotland....

Not sure what weeds and vegetables she'll be able to grow over there.

July

What a great spell of growing weather we've had (ie it's rained a lot)! I know, a lot of you would have preferred it drier, but for us gardeners it's great not having to water the garden! The vegetables have been enjoying the warm days we've had, too.

Of course I wrote this blog before the dry spell we're having just now, so I eventually had to go out and water the vegetables after all...

Everything is looking lush and green and I'll soon be able to start harvesting my first courgettes (from the greenhouse) and my first onions. I have already started picking some huge, juicy strawberries. Sorry, but they won't be for sale in the shop - they're destined to be made into strawberry wine and jam, with a little help from our next wwoofer who arrives with us soon!

Who knew chickens like to eat cabbage? Well, I noticed our

cabbages were looking a bit tatty - it looked like they had been nibbled at the edges, so I checked for caterpillars, but couldn't find any sign of them.

While I was there, along came one of our chickens and, bold as brass, started munching away at my cabbages!! So, I've had to build a frame to keep the chickens out. As an added benefit, it also helps shelter the cabbages from the wind, something these Brussels sprouts are not particularly fond of either.

The chickens are still doing fine. They don't lay as many eggs as they used to, but hey, they are ex-battery so what can we expect?!

The other day, one hen in particular looked very poorly and lethargic. So, I put her in a cat carrier, isolating her from the other chickens and delved into my books and searched online to see if I could find out what might be causing her to feel unwell.

I think she had something called 'crop bound' which means that she couldn't shift the food in her crop and felt very uncomfortable. For treatment it suggested administering olive oil with a plastic syringe (the pharmacist had a good laugh when I told her what I was going to use it for!).

Anyway, I left her in the cat carrier overnight and looked in on her the following morning. She didn't look any better to me, so I left her with just water for the day (after all, I had to go to work) and hoped she would perk up during my absence.

Well, when I came back that night, there was a right racket coming from inside that carrier. I could tell she was back to her old (annoying) self again. One can only imagine what she was trying to say, I got the impression it wasn't very nice... good job I can't speak 'chicken'!

Did you know...

... chickens can live up to **8 years**? 'Muffy' the oldest chicken ever recorded lived to the ripe old age of 22! That's an awfully long time to have a chicken follow you about the garden!

August

It's been so warm last month that everything in the garden has just 'shot up'.

The soft fruit crop has been so good I've got strawberries coming out of my ears and raspberries out of my... er, nose! You won't find me complaining though - I've been able to make lots of strawberry jam, strawberry wine and strawberry ice cream (from the leftover pulp), which was delicious and especially welcome given the soaring temperatures we've had.

As usual the swedes and turnips have been doing well. That's the one vegetable which never fails - even in that dreadful summer we had two years ago, we still had a successful crop of swedes and turnips.

In Spring I got a bit over-excited with my planting and now the greenhouse looks more like a tropical rainforest! I thought there would be enough space so I planted 20 tomatoes; 10 cucumbers; 3 aubergines; 10 beans of various shapes; 3 pumpkins; 1 watermelon (the result of an experiment with some seeds carried out by our neighbours) and a variety of sweet and chilli peppers planted in pots on the greenhouse floor.

The plants look fabulous; the only problem is it's so dense in there that it's proving difficult to harvest anything.

The chickens are still hanging on in there; chasing our cat (and us!) and eating caterpillars. I had to take my chicken-cabbage-protection down, so they could get in and eat the caterpillars off the cabbage leaves. No doubt about it, these chickens do come in useful sometimes!

September

Suddenly it's September and that means harvesting and preserving fresh vegetables as well as eating them, of course. For the first time since we planted our pear tree, it's producing a decent amount of fruit. They are small Dutch cooking pears which turn red when cooked and are especially delicious in winter. This variety is called 'Gieser Wildeman' and if you are interested, we got our tree from the garden centre in Tillicoultry. Believe it or not, the owners are also Dutch so they will know exactly what you are talking about if you are looking for this variety!

Sometimes lack of time can reap amazing results in gardening! We haven't paid much attention to one of the cabbage beds for some time, causing it to overgrow a little bit. But it looks really attractive now with an abundance of wild flowers, some nasturtiums and above all, very healthy looking cabbages. All we had to do was just pick off a few caterpillars. The butterflies either couldn't find the cabbages hidden between the flowers, or the chickens got to the caterpillars before we could!

Either way, the white cabbages are now so big that we are able to make an extra batch of sauerkraut to keep us going during the colder winter months.

Now some sad news... we have lost one of our chickens. We are not really sure if it went broody again and is fiercely protecting a clutch of goodness knows how many eggs somewhere, or if nature has stepped in and she has finally been gobbled up by a fox.

Of course we hope it's not the latter, but we have searched everywhere and she is still nowhere to be found. I don't think we'll ever clap eyes on her again.

October

It feels a bit silly to be writing my blog in the first week of September, but my husband and I are off on our travels, touring Europe for the last two weeks of September! Still, a few things have already happened in such a short space of time...

The runaway chicken has done it again! Just one day after I had sent the last newsletter, our neighbour found it sitting outside her front door and brought it back (the chicken, that is, not her front door!). The chicken had been missing for nearly four weeks - and naturally we had feared the worst! Needless to say, she wasn't in the best of health and I've been trying to nurse her back to full health with (poultry) multivitamins, (poultry) probiotics and a lot of TLC. She was admitted to our 'chicken hospital' (aka the porch) for a few nights but has since been discharged and is now enjoying her recovery in a fenced off part of the garden.

The 20 tomato plants we planted are really paying off! I can't believe how many tomatoes we've got! Literally kilos and kilos! I suppose this means I've got to make lots of passata and tomato sauce to keep us going over winter and beyond...

I still haven't made up my mind about 'biodynamic' gardening. Last year I tried to garden as much as I could following the biodynamic calendar and those vegetables I did grow this way seemed more resistant to disease... or perhaps it was just my imagination, I'm not too sure. I am convinced, however, that every year a different vegetable or fruit will perform better than others.

Last year, for example, we had lots of beans: runner beans; dried beans and French beans, so last year was definitely a 'bean year'. Unfortunately this year the beans have not been as prolific as last year, but the fruit-bearing vegetables have performed really well: tomatoes, pears, cucumbers and soft fruit plants all yielded loads more fruit. So this would seem to suggest that this year is a 'fruit year'.

Have any of our readers out there experienced anything similar? It would be nice to compare notes and test out my theory...

November

I hate to tell you that one of our chickens passed away after a short illness. After nursing 'the runaway chicken' back to health, another one fell ill. I tried to give her a foul smelling remedy made from mashed up garlic, chilli pepper, carrot and turmeric for a week but to no avail. It's a bit sad really, because she was named 'The one who considered herself to be my friend' and would sit next to me on our garden bench and wait patiently on the back door step for me to appear.

At least she lived the last year of her life with the freedom to run around in our garden and the fields beyond. Still, a real shame - I'll miss her.

It's always nice to look back at the gardening year in November and, all in all, I had a really good year. Probably everyone who grows their own vegetables and fruit had a productive summer.

Fruits have done especially well, particularly my raspberries - which even produced a second crop of fruit in October, albeit a small one!

The freezer is bursting with runner beans, tomato soup and pureed tomatoes. And the larder is stacked full with pickles (around 10 jars of pickled gherkins!); jam; various vegetables in mustard sauce; chilli sauce and tomato ketchup. Oh and of course around 5kg of sauerkraut! More than enough to keep us going during the cold winter months ahead!

Finally, the pond liner is in. Hooray! My husband and I are having a bet on how quickly it will fill up with rain water. I think it'll be full to the brim by Christmas, but my husband thinks it won't be full until after January. But if the recent wet weather is anything to go by, I think the odds are good that I'm going to win. If I do, it means he'll have to cook me a lavish Christmas dinner with all the trimmings!

December

Not much has been happening in the garden to be honest. I'm busy harvesting cabbages, brussels sprouts and paksoi, so the freezer is still chock-a-block with frozen vegetables. Ah well, the cold winter months are just around the corner and we'll hopefully have enough vegetables and preserves to last us right through to March, when the edible weeds start growing and our kale and endive do too.

I've also cleared up the greenhouse and shed, so that it is all neat and tidy - in preparation for when I start sowing again.

Clearing out the greenhouse I encountered a rather large spider (HUGE in other words). I got such a fright I nearly wet my plants! There were probably hundreds more but thankfully I only came face to face with this one. Even this one, was one too many! You know what they say: 'They are probably more afraid of you than you are of them.' Er, no. Well, this big spider seemed to be saying, 'What do you want?! I'm just minding my own business here, so beat it and leave me alone. Or else....'

So that's exactly what I did! I'm not afraid of mice, snakes or any other animal, but spiders definitely give me the 'heebie-jeebies'!

I have decided to rename one of our hens. The chicken formerly referred to as the 'Runaway Chicken' shall henceforth be known as 'The Hooligan'. Mainly due to her yob-like, anti-social behaviour - shouting and swearing at us if we don't let her out of the coop when it suits her. Don't ask me to repeat what she says, it's far too shocking!

The other three hens are doing fine, filling the days fighting off the neighbours' new chickens; chasing our cats; getting rid of any unwanted garden pests and plotting to take over the world

Well, one of those statements isn't strictly true. But which one?

Oak Leaves Eleven

January

I still can't believe we're now into 2015!

We had the first proper snowfall mid December and it was so funny to watch our bewildered, reluctant hens venture out of their run into a world covered with snow (well, our garden at least!).

An hour or so after feeding the chickens, we opened the hatch for them to go outside. 'The Hooligan' wasn't too sure about it all and stood in the doorway, blocking it. I could see her thinking to herself: "What the…? This was green yesterday, now it's white! Not sure if this is safe."

After hesitating for a while, she plucked (unfortunate choice of words, there!) up enough courage and slowly took a step outside with the rest following cautiously behind her. The hens came to a halt again next to the shed, before venturing further out into the garden. After a while they seemed to get the hang of it!

Our two cats really liked the winter wonderland as well - they even went ice skating, gliding over the surface of the pond which had frozen over. I wish I had time to fetch my camera and take a picture, but it was fun just to watch their antics. A little later our oldest cat decided to have another go - fortunately for him he first tested the ice with a tentative paw - and a good job, too because by that time the ice had melted!

We're certain to get even more snow and ice in the next few months, so I'll make sure I've got my camera ready this time!

February

Dear, oh dear, oh dear... what a lot of snow we've had - not to mention high winds!

For the first time since 2012 I had to ask a colleague to fill in for me at the shop because I was completely snowed in! I set off with high hopes, only to grind to a halt 50 yards from the house! A 3 foot high snowdrift blocked the only path down to the main road!

The first thing I did was dig a path for the chickens, but they all looked so cold, fed up and miserable that I decided to lock them in their run (after I had finished clearing the snow out of that as well!).

Luckily our super sturdy greenhouse didn't suffer any damage in the high winds and we didn't lose any slates from our roof, either. Not one.

We are still eating our own home-grown vegetables, only now it's in preserved form: sauerkraut, pickled red cabbage, vegetables in mustard and dried beans. It feels great to still have all this left to eat. We have the wwoofers who helped us over the summer to thank for this. Without their help, we'd never have been able to harvest so much!

Believe it or not, the first wwoofers of 2015 have already been booked in! Talk about being well-organized...

March

I know I say this a lot, but... wow!

We recently had a visit from George Anderson (presenter), Shona (the director) and Callum (the gardener) from BBC's 'The Beechgrove Garden'!

A popular item on the show involves 'The Beechgrove Garden' experts helping with any problems viewers experience in the garden. So I wrote in a while back asking about my apple trees hoping they would be able to give me some advice on which variety to grow or if there was anything else they suggest I do to make the trees 'happier'. I got a phone call a little while after, informing me that my garden had joined the shortlist of possible projects which may feature in the next series of 'The Beechgrove Garden'. But before all that, we were told George Anderson would be coming over for a wee chat (and a cup of tea as it happened!).

We don't know yet if we will make it to the small screen, but we had a lovely time with George, Shona and Callum. George is very knowledgeable and gave us a lot of advice. Not just about apple trees, but also about pruning, which type of soil to use etc. They were all lovely people, so even if we are not chosen to appear on the show, we still spent a very pleasant hour together!

The hens are not laying at the moment. Maybe they're getting too old for that kind of nonsense (after all, they are supposed to be retired!), but occasionally we do get a rather ugly looking 'wrinkled' egg. The other day I found one which didn't look like it had been produced by one of our hens at all - more like one of those alien eggs you see in the 'Alien' movies. The ones with the 'face huggers' inside! Maybe one of our neighbours' hens sneaked in and laid her egg in our nest box! But then again, our neighbours probably say the same thing about ours. These hens are a right bunch!

Perhaps she simply got confused. One of our neighbours' hens is very similar in appearance to ours, so we decided to wrap a pink ring around our hen's leg to avoid any confusion. This makes it easier when it comes time to lock our hens in at night and we don't accidentally lock in the wrong one!

April

Great news! Not long after I had finished last month's blog we were informed we would be filmed for 'The Beechgrove Garden' after all - probably sometime in May!! If ever there was a good time to use the word 'wow!' it's now! So... Wow! More on this a little later..

We are nearing the end of the home grown vegetables we grew last year. No more sauerkraut, vegetables in mustard sauce or pickled red cabbage. All gone.

A pity, but to be honest I'm really looking forward to eating fresh produce again! Luckily we have a greenhouse full of endive (courtesy of my husband, who thinks it's the best vegetable... ever!) and also curly kale, which I sowed later in the year. I'm also looking forward to the turnip tops and lettuce I sowed at the beginning of March.

And that's the new season off to a start! I'm so excited!!

Besides the one wrinkly egg we get every other day, a tiny wee, mini-egg appeared out-of-the-blue one day! Not sure what the hen must've thought after laying it, probably something like "Is this all I've got to show for all that hard work?"

Or maybe it was the Hooligan's way of telling us: "That's all you're getting today... should've let me out of the coop when I wanted!!"

We never know exactly which hen lays which egg, but most of them seem happy now they are living a better life with us (apart from 'The Hooligan' of course, who thinks it's all too good to be true!).

As I mentioned, the good folks from BBC's 'The Beechgrove Garden' will be visiting us next month to film in our garden. We've been having some problems growing fruit trees - are they too exposed? Too wet? Not the right variety? 'The Beechgrove

Garden' crew are coming over to help us plant the right trees and give us the benefit of their knowledge, experience and expertise.

It will take a full day to film something that will only appear on TV for about 5 or 6 minutes! That's how long these things take apparently, unless they anticipate me mucking up my lines and having to do take after take after take?!

I don't know yet when it will be aired, but as soon as I've got a date I'll let you know!

To read the whole, unedited '**The Beechgrove Garden**' saga turn to page 173. There was just so much to write about this extra-ordinary experience, I couldn't fit it all in the pages of May's newsletter!

May

We now know the date our garden is going to feature on BBC2's 'The Beechgrove Garden'.

Tune in to BBC2 Scotland on Thursday 21st May at 7.30pm (the programme is repeated on BBC2 London on Sunday 24th May at 9.00am).*

It's not going to be about growing apples as we first thought, though.

When George Anderson and the programme's director visited us recently we told them our plans for the back garden, which involved creating a bog area to make the most of the excess water

* *This was back in 2015 of course.*

from our newly built pond. This must've piqued their interest because the production team decided it would be a better idea to help us create a bog garden in our back garden instead! Not quite what we originally had in mind - perhaps they thought it'd make for better TV, who knows?

Who knew chickens could get lice? We didn't, that's for sure. Until, that is, we noticed one hen in particular looking a bit off-colour and upon further inspection discovered that her feathers were infested by wee white creepy crawlies. These lice don't like humans, they only live on poultry and can only be transferred from bird to bird. That's probably how she got them in the first place.

Anyway, we powdered the hens with some sort of non-toxic clay to kill the lice. Of course, 'The Hooligan' was the most difficult one to treat - what a fuss she made! Couldn't have been that bad, though, because she's back to laying eggs again!

We are still recovering from the shock, though!

Unfortunately, the lice infestation proved too much for one of our hens and she sadly passed away. We laid her to rest under the hawthorn tree. That now leaves only three chickens (of the original five we rescued), but we are thinking of getting 3 or 4 hardier 'Black Rock' chickens from down the road, to boost their numbers.

Growing season is in full swing again, with all my windowsills brimming with seedlings. All the usual suspects are there: tomatoes, peppers, sprouts, flowers, beans and peas to name but a few.

June

I hope many of you managed to catch 'The Beechgrove Garden' on BBC2 the other day. It was very surreal to see ourselves on the small screen. It felt as though we were watching a home video. The chickens (especially 'The Hooligan') were the real stars of the show though! My husband and I had great fun planting, filming and getting advice from George Anderson and luckily I don't think I messed up too much in front of the camera. Although it was quite difficult to appear and act 'natural'.

As for growing vegetables... needless to say, nothing has grown much because of the cold weather we've had. I even had to buy cabbage plants after my original seedlings died off, but they've died too because of the dreadful cold and windy weather we've had. The greenhouse is once again bursting with seedlings waiting to go out, but I think I'll hold on a bit longer for the winds to die down.

The first wwoofer has arrived, so we'll get cracking with planting out that massive pond, our 'vision' and 'smell' borders and perhaps the 'medicinal' garden if we have time.

We'll also be making spring oak leaf wine and sweet cicely wine, which will be ready to enjoy in a few months. And of course, we'll be making elderflower champagne for when the weather finally warms up. If it ever warms up!

The pond is starting to look good, we've just planted some irises I got from one of our suppliers and hopefully my husband and new wwoofer will be planting lots of other water plants in the next few days. Unfortunately I can't give them a hand since I'm working in the shop all this week, covering for staff holidays.

After our appearance on **'The Beechgrove Garden'** I alter the title of my blog accordingly and change it to 'Josine's Garden, Chicken and **Bog** Blog'. It remains unchanged for 30 issues!

July

What a difference a rise in temperature can make to the garden! Plants suddenly start to grow and produce flowers. Bees, bumblebees and butterflies suddenly appear and in general, everything looks so much better - more colourful, more vibrant!

The Beechgrove's bog garden is starting to look good too. We've now got yellow and purple flowers and the pond is particularly popular with the swallows. You can see them swooping down over it to catch insects.

The 'five senses' garden is taking shape as well. The 'smell' and 'vision' borders have been planted out, so now we've just got to be patient and wait for the plants to grow!

Vegetables of course are growing too, although all my cabbages are really slow off the mark this year. My neighbours have had the same problem, so I guess I'll just have to put it down to the cold May we've just had.

This year I've decided to grow garlic on ridges. When driving through France last September, my husband and I noticed that garlic was growing on ridges there. Knowing that the French are famous for using garlic in everything (and any garlic I've grown never grew beyond an inch in diameter) I thought I'd give it a try. So last year I made some ridges and planted the cloves in them. So far, so good... the stems look a lot better than they have done in previous years, but of course I won't know for sure until I harvest them towards the end of August.

One of our chickens is beginning to show signs of old age, I'm afraid. She's so stiff and lame that she occasionally needs help getting in and out of her hen house (which is off the ground and is only accessible via a ramp). Apparently even chickens can get arthritis! She still has a healthy appetite and drinks well, though. Out of our three chickens we now only get one egg per week if we are lucky!

Anyway, these ladies don't need to 'work' any longer - they are retired after all!

Just as I was putting the finishing touches to this month's blog, that particular chicken has since bounced back and is behaving more like her normal self again! Phew! Great news!

August

Tell me this... I'm just curious... just what exactly happened to Summer? Did I blink and miss it this year? We've had gales, heavy rain and flooding and all of that in the middle of July! Needless to say, the vegetables are not doing much in the way of growing. For the first time in over 14 months we had to buy vegetables from the supermarket - can you believe it? The lettuces I sowed some months ago still only have a few leaves and the swedes and turnips are absolutely tiny.

We had to support our 'Dutch kapucijner' peas with props to protect them against the latest storm which saw wind speeds of up to 40mph.

Miraculously, the whole structure survived.

Not sure if the pumpkins we planted will come to anything, they're growing up against a structure which might be familiar to some - it's the shop's old herb rack!

Strangely enough the strawberries are ripening despite the lack of sunshine. They do taste a bit watery though, so it will be interesting to see if this affects the wine we make from them. Our new wwoofer (from the USA) is very excited about making home-made wine (and drinking it, too of course!). Although being from California she doesn't appreciate the present climate much... Well, at least there are lots of wines and jams to make this coming week to keep us busy and take our minds off the weather. As well as strawberries, we've also got red currants, black currants and hopefully some gooseberries, too.

Despite all the rain we've had, there is one part of the garden that's thriving; The Beechgrove Garden's bog area of course! The plants love it! Actually all newly planted plants quite like the rain, it makes them settle better.

Never mind the plants, though - I could do with a bit of sunshine!

My husband and I tried to rescue a pheasant chick the other day from the clutches of our cat. We caught him playing with it and managed to frighten him away so that he dropped the bird and allowed us to take it away from him. We made a nice cosy 'nest' with straw and sheep's wool, put water and chicken mash in the box and put it over a warm radiator. The chick seemed pretty lively, but sadly it didn't survive the night. We were actually quite upset about that...

Now, if only one of the hens was broody, we could have placed the chick under the hen in the hope that she would raise it as her own. But unfortunately it was not to be...

September

Hooray! We've got 5 new chickens to keep 'The Hooligan' company.

Unfortunately... 'The Hooligan' can't stand them! She still thinks she's the top dog (or more correctly, hen), the first in the pecking order and she's determined to let the five new ones (which I've named 'The Chick-Peas') know all about it.

Luckily we've enough space to keep them all out of each other's way, so 'The Hooligan' isn't able to pick on the new arrivals as much as she'd like. My husband chose the breed of chicken this time, called 'Black Rocks'. They are super hardy, have long legs and apparently can become quite affectionate over time. 'The Hooligan' has wasted no time in teaching them bad habits, though - like showing them how to gain entry into the house. So now when I get home, I've got 10 (!) chickens trailing after me

('The Hooligan', 5 Chick-Peas and 4 of our neighbours' hens).

And to top it all, they're not even laying eggs yet! What a bunch of spoiled fowl they are!

Harvest is in full swing now with everything ripening.

This year has been a complete mixed bag on the vegetable front - a few success stories, but just as many failures. My potatoes and onions have done really well and the Dutch 'kapucijner' peas have filled up a whole gardening tub. But the rest of the beans have performed really, really badly. I've got about 5 runner beans, 1 French bean and (if I'm lucky) two handfuls of peas. Pitiful! The courgettes haven't done much either, despite being under a cloche.

Although the tomatoes are ripening, I haven't got half the amount I had this time last year. Worryingly the same goes for the cucumbers and the gherkins, too.

To top it all I had a really bad infestation of aphids and what I think are whitefly in the greenhouse. Spraying them with soapy water didn't help much - it only succeeded in weakening the plants.

If everything goes well, though, I might be lucky enough to get one squash and maybe one sweet pepper this year! Oh the joys...

For some odd reason I couldn't lay my hands on my October 2015 Garden Blog (the chickens probably ate it!), so let's pretend there wasn't very much to write about that month and skip ahead to November!

November

Ooohhh, they are in so much trouble! 'The Chick-Peas' (our 5 new chickens) are still not laying any eggs, but are successfully destroying my vegetables in the meantime! They seem to have taken a liking to our leafy vegetables, so the curly kale, paksoi, chard and everything else has been nibbled on (or worse still, ripped to shreds).

Unfortunately, we bought them from what we thought was a reputable supplier as 'point-of-lay' chickens, which means they should start laying within two weeks or so. Nope, not this lot.

I looked online at pictures of how our chickens should look (if they were the age we were told they were when we got them) and discovered that our lot are only maybe 11 to 12 weeks old and chickens won't start laying eggs until they are at least 20 weeks! We're lucky if we get any eggs before Easter, never mind Christmas! Looks like there won't be any pickled eggs this year!

On the plus side they are very cute and are able to jump up onto the windowsill so they can peek inside the house!

This year I've decided to conduct a little experiment... growing trees from seeds. When visiting Scone Palace Gardens the other day, I collected some acorns, pine cones and ash seeds.

I'll sow the seeds in pots and hopefully they will germinate and grow into a tree... eventually. Of course I'll have to be very patient as trees don't grow in a day, but hopefully I'll be able to sit in the shade of the oak tree I planted in the back of my garden when I retire!

But the way I look at it is this: this is my legacy to the future - more trees in the area I once lived in.

Preserving wise, I have been making 'Atjar Tjampoer' from my own home grown white cabbage, onions, carrots and bean sprouts (shop bought). I just love this Indonesian/Dutch dish! When I was a child my mum had to stop me from finishing off the whole jar in one sitting. Now I can make my own and eat as much of it as I like, without being told off!

> On page 185 you will find my recipe for making **'Atjar Tjampoer'**.

December

Aw... poor old 'The Hooligan'.

She is now officially our last remaining chicken!

I tried... but I just couldn't persuade my husband to keep any of the 'Black Rocks'. So, sadly he returned them to the breeder we got them from. Although we were originally told that they were approaching point-of-lay, that can mean anything from 1 week to 2 years! We can't wait that long for our eggs, so... back into the run they went, waiting to be sold to the next lot of eejits who came along!

Don't worry. 'The Hooligan' isn't lonely. During the day she hangs out with the neighbours' chickens. It's just at night that she is all alone in the hen house and has no one to huddle up against to keep warm. So, if the weather gets too cold, we're going to tuck her into a pet carrier, make her all cosy and warm and keep her indoors during the night. We've had the first snow fall the other day, a reminder that winter isn't that far away...

I have to say 'The Beechgrove's Bog garden' is looking pretty good. The wet summer weather has been great for allowing the plants to establish. We've planted more plants in our 'Five Senses' border and the 'scent' and 'vision' area has been planted out as well. It's truly amazing how much difference a few months can make!

I don't mind telling you that I'm pleasantly surprised by the size of my root vegetables this year! By mid July I thought most of the harvest had refused to grow at all and anything that had grown would probably end up just rotting away. But to my utter amazement I've started harvesting carrots, turnips and parsnips and they are actually very healthy looking. So, I'm pretty chuffed! Carrots, onions and potatoes make a great Dutch dish. You just boil them all together and mash them up afterwards. We Dutch - what are we like? We do love our mashed potatoes with vegetables. Any vegetable! We are a simple people!

2016

Four Berries and a Festival

January

For the second month running, poor old 'The Hooligan'.

She went through a terrible moult (most chickens do at some point) and became so malnourished and weak that she could hardly walk! Now, I know what you're thinking: "Look after that poor chicken!"

Believe me, we have been, honest... but we didn't know until now that moulting can cause problems with walking too. Thanks to the internet I pretty soon realised that all 'The Hooligan' needed was protein.

So, that's exactly what she got: cat food (dry and wet varieties); wild bird seeds (I told her it's really only for birds, but she reminded me that technically she is a bird, too!) and dried mealworms (delicious!). Within two days of putting her on this luxury diet, she looked (and started behaving) more like her old self again. Jumping up at me, flapping, shouting at me and generally behaving badly like her name suggests - a right hooligan! In other words, back to normal.

Now her feathers have grown back and she looks like a proper lady again (of course she's got a taste for her new diet and doesn't want to go back to eating chicken pellets again!).

What a wet winter we've had so far. This surely must be the wettest December ever?!

Needless to say, the bog garden loves it, but the rest of the garden not so much. As a matter of fact, you could say we've got an extra two 'new' bog gardens now!

Being in Glendevon means that we've had about 3 inches of snow lying for a couple of days already. Luckily I was well prepared and harvested plenty of root vegetables to see us through. It's surprising how well they stay in the ground despite being submerged in this newly formed 'pond'.

February

Not much to write about this month. We've had 4 inches of snow which lay for a week and a half, but that's all melted away now and we're back to the usual wet and windy weather. Oh joy!

But I have the sneaky feeling we've not seen the last of the snow. February is the coldest month of the year after all!

I'm not sure what to do with 'The Hooligan'; she's not behaving like a hooligan any more! She no longer shouts and curses at me, in fact she now tweets and chirps like a sweet little canary!

Maybe it's time to give her a new name?

Mind you, when my husband and I were on 'bum cleaning' duty (chickens regularly get dirty bottoms and it's best to clean it before it gets out of hand) she was more like her old self again - kicking and cursing at us for dumping her in a basin of soapy water and giving her a good old scrub. She's back to looking her very best again though, but she doesn't have access to a mirror, so she can't see the difference herself.

As there are no other chickens in 'her' flock left, maybe she no longer feels the need to prove herself. I think she sees herself as one flock now and the neighbours' chickens as a different one.

She still follows me around, which is very cute...most of the time. When my husband and I recently came back from a weekend away, she was the first one to come running up to the car and greet us, long before our cats decided to put in an appearance! She also likes to overtake me when I'm walking towards the shed. It's where the bird food is kept you see, so I have an inkling that might be why. She even managed to pop out an egg on the first day it snowed, which surprised us all - not least of all her!

Our neighbours up the hill keep chickens too, but they also have a cockerel. So hopefully if they get chicks in spring, we'll be able to 'adopt' some too. Or maybe we'll incubate some fertile eggs ourselves in spring. We haven't made our minds up yet...

March

Forget everything I said about 'The Hooligan' in last month's newsletter (the bit about her not behaving like a hooligan any longer). She's back to her (good?) old self again - you know, shouting and swearing like a trooper. She's even been teaching the neighbours' chickens some of her more colourful vocabulary! What is she like?!

Even at the ripe old age of four (and a bit) she's started laying eggs again - so she must be one happy chicken.

Recently, when our neighbours' son was looking after their chickens, he somehow managed to lock 'The Hooligan' in their henhouse by mistake. She must've liked it there because the next night we were chicken-less! Maybe she thought the neighbours' henhouse was more homely. Who knows? Thanks for that 'The Hooligan'... that's gratitude for you!

But by the third night she was back home again. Maybe she thought it was too noisy there, too crowded, too warm? Or maybe she preferred the solitude of our place?? Only she knows for sure...

Garden wise, I've been sowing my tomatoes (5 different varieties!), chilli peppers and aubergines. I've never really been able to grow decent sized aubergines and to tell you the truth, I don't even like them that much! But it's just something I want to be able to succeed in growing some day.

We're still eating vegetables grown by ourselves, like carrots, kale, potatoes and onions and we've still got our preserved vegetables like atjar tjampoer, chutney and sauerkraut.

It's getting a wee bit on the boring side to be honest, but it won't be long until I can pick some weeds from the garden to add a dash of green to our meals. Things like nettles and sorrel are usually available to pick early and you can make delicious, warming soups from them.

April

April is upon us, which hopefully means the start of warm, sunny days, daffodils and lambs. Mind you, if you're like me and live next to a field with sheep and have to listen to these adorable little things bleating all night, they might not seem so cute for very long!

In the garden this year I'm trying the 'no dig gardening' approach, which means, er, no digging. In the garden. Hooray!

Basically all you have to do is this: weed the beds, put compost on top and leave it as it is. Simple. Apparently the worms and other little creepy crawlies will pull the nutrients into the ground, therefore enriching the soil. Also, if you think about it, in nature there is no-one there to dig over the soil! And most of the nutrients and beneficial bacteria are in the first 5cm (2 inches) of the soil anyway, so digging it over will only mean you are pushing all this goodness deep down into the soil. It does make sense I suppose.

My five different tomato varieties are coming up nicely, it's obvious some are doing much better than others, but we'll wait and see what happens. A lot about gardening involves waiting, biding your time, being patient. I have started harvesting my very first fresh greens from the greenhouse and some weeds from the garden. It's just so nice to have something green (and something other than a root vegetable) at tea-time! I have winter purslane, kale and chard and in a couple of weeks, my husband's favourite, endive from the greenhouse. I sowed them back in the autumn, and they germinated before the cold weather set in. They went into hibernation during the shorter days and suddenly sprang back into life once the weather started to warm up and the days got longer. Isn't 'Mother Nature' simply magical?!

'The Hooligan' is still going strong. I'm surprised she comes back to us every night, although she now goes to bed earlier than the neighbours' chickens. Perhaps it's something to do with her age - she is getting on, you know!

It's a shame, though... she has poultry lice again. Not only do the little critters irritate her, we also have to wash her, ahem, 'derriere' regularly and then powder her with this sort of clay stuff (non toxic of course!) which is meant to kill the lice. Having to do this on 'The Hooligan' is very challenging to say the least, due to her temperament. But she always gets a few treats afterwards as a reward. Yep, she is one spoilt little chicken!

> Okay... you might need to go grab some tissues before reading May's blog. Don't say I didn't warn you!

May

It is with a heavy heart that I have to tell you that, sadly, Stirling's most famous chicken passed away mid April.

'The Hooligan' (aka 'Hooly El Bully') caught an infection and due to her age (and the fact she was an ex-battery hen), she simply didn't have the strength to fight it this time. She was just too weak. She has been the star of this blog for some time now and we will miss her dearly. She is the only chicken to get a wee memorial in our garden to mark where she is buried. She certainly was special - and a bit of a celebrity after all!

So, here's a short-ish story about her life with us.

"In September 2013 we re-homed 5 ex-battery chickens. When they arrived, their combs were pale and floppy and they were missing quite a few feathers on their chests. They also had to learn how to scratch (from scratch!) and had probably never seen or felt sunlight before. It was pretty clear from the start that there was one chicken that ruled the roost. It's normal for there to be a pecking order and the other chickens just knew to stay out of her way. She had a very loud voice and made sure she told us off for keeping her locked in the chicken coop for too long. That's why we decided to name her, rather appropriately, 'The Hooligan'.

When, after two years, she was the last one left standing, we decided to get 5 more chickens. To keep her company.

Younger ones, this time - chickens that would keep laying eggs for some years to come. I kid you not; 'The Hooligan' took to wrecking the place while the 5 new arrivals (or 'Chick Peas' as we called them) cowered in a corner, huddled together, trembling. When, after 8 weeks, the 'Chick Peas' still hadn't shown any signs of approaching point of lay, my husband returned them and 'The Hooligan' was left on her own once again. Relative peace and tranquillity returned...

With all her adventures and her fondness for using 'inappropriate' language, she soon became the star of the newsletter blog. Sadly in mid April she caught another infection and although she had survived quite a few in the past, she just wasn't strong enough to shake this one off this time.

We buried her in our garden and planted a special sign to mark her grave which reads: 'Here lies 'The Hooligan' Stirling's most famous chicken.' She would've liked that.

Word must have spread amongst the local wildlife, because in no time at all a male pheasant came to audition for the vacancy of 'The New Hooligan'. He must've heard the position came with its own Twitter account and guaranteed celebrity status! I don't know what 'The Hooligan' has been telling every bird in the glen, but we don't particularly need another one! Anyway, to us, she was irreplaceable. One of a kind. Unique.

The scary thing is, however, some time ago I spoke to one of my customers (let's call him Mr T), who was in the process of moving house with his wife (better call her Mrs T!). They were looking for a reliable person to look after the 6 chickens they had. I was more than happy to re-home their chickens once the sale of their house had gone through. The very next day after 'The Hooligan' died Mr T came to the shop to say that I could collect them any time, because they had sold their house. I mean... what are the chances of that?!

So, here we are, proud owners of a rare breed of chickens known as 'Scots Dumpies' which we've named 'The Hurkies and the

Other One'.

All I can say is that even after just one week they seem extremely well behaved: they perch, lay their eggs in the designated nest boxes (managing not to break them!); they go to bed early and generally show impeccable manners.

More to follow in next month's newsletter!

> ### Did you know...
> ... 4th May is **Star Wars Day**, as in: "May the 4th (force) be with you." If you're a Star Wars fan, I bet you already knew that and celebrate it accordingly!

June

May kicked off with some glorious sunshine and everything is catching up in the garden.

But what a strange spring it has been! The last day of April we had a snow coverage of 10cm (4 inches), and 9 days later the temperatures soared to 20°C! That was a bit of a shock to the system. One minute I was wearing a winter jacket and gloves and the next short sleeves and sun cream - all in the space of over a week!

Then mid May we had a late frost, but this time I was ready for it. I invested in some horticultural fleece to protect my flowering pear tree from late frost and it arrived just in time to cover the tree from head to toe (or should that be branch to root?). Let's hope we'll get more than one miserable pear this year.

The big success story over the winter months has been the kale and chard I left over winter in the greenhouse. But also the cauliflower I left over winter in the garden has been a great success. I finally managed to grow reasonable sized cauliflowers which I'm pretty proud of! It's a variety called 'May Star' and you sow it in September, leave the young plants in the garden over winter (they need a cool period, so don't cover them!) and then come March you can either cover them (to let the plants mature) and they should be ready for harvest in May. If you choose not to cover them they should still grow, but might not be ready to harvest until later.

And on the chicken front... The new arrivals are extremely pleasant; they are fun to watch; perch the way chickens are supposed to do; use the nest boxes for laying eggs; eat grubs and generally make very funny noises. They now also seem to recognise me: I'm the one who digs up worms (whilst weeding) or feeds them seeds. So, they tend to come running towards me as soon as they hear or see me, which is kind of cute, but not very handy if you are trying to weed and there are 6 nosey chickens flapping around your feet.

We've also come up with another name for them: 'Houdini and the Hurkies'.

Basically, Houdini is the only non-'Scots Dumpie' (possibly a 'Black Rock'), but because she is bigger than the rest, she rules the roost! And she's a real escape artist. If she finds a hole in the fencing, she'll 'escape' (a la famous escapologist Harry Houdini, only a female version), urging 'The Hurkies' to follow her.

The name 'Hurkies' comes from the Dutch word for squatting down, 'hurken'. And because of their short legs, it does look like the chickens spend most of their time squatting down, so I thought it sounded quite appropriate.

July

'Three Sisters', warm weather, cold weather and broody hens...

Er, climate change anyone? The start of the month was really hot, with temperatures as high as 25°C and dry for weeks on end. All my water butts were empty and I feared for the bog garden plants. They don't like the weather to be too dry, you see.

Then the weather turned and temperatures dipped (almost overnight) to only 11°C. Not only was this a bit of a shock to us, it took the garden by surprise, too!

This year I'm practising the 'Three Sisters' method of growing vegetables - a method developed by Native Americans. You grow corn, runner beans and pumpkins all at the same spot in the garden. The corn provides support for the runner beans, the runner beans provide nitrogen for the corn and the pumpkin keeps everything cool and moist thanks to their large leaves.

But of course, this being Scotland, the corn just can't keep up with the runner beans, so we still have to stake them. Corn gets pollinated by wind, which shouldn't be a problem where we are, with the constant high winds we experience up here. Although the pumpkin is growing very, very slowly right now.

The potatoes, however, are looking very healthy. We stored some of last year's harvest to plant again this year and so far, so good. I'm growing 'Cara', 'Robinta' and 'Sarpo Mira', the latter two varieties I grew last year.

Bless them, our lovely new hens... one of 'The Hurkies' has gone all broody on us!

This means she will sit on an egg waiting for it to hatch. Or if there isn't an egg to sit on, she'll just sit there anyway, as if she *was* sitting on an egg waiting for it to hatch! Even without a cockerel, hens can still get broody. Some can be quite vicious and protective, too, so better watch out! Our neighbours' wee bantams (aka wee, wee tiny hens) are also feeling broody just now and they'll peck anyone who dares come near them.

Not our 'Hurky' though, she just mutters, "Stay away or else..." she is such a softy!

I enquired about fertilized 'Scots Dumpy' eggs from a fella who lives nearby, but he no longer keeps 'Scots Dumpies' because they are too difficult to breed due to the gene which gives them their distinctive short legs. So, we've decided to try and get this particular hen out of her broodiness by lifting her off the nest, taking away the eggs, putting her next to her food, closing the nest box etc. But... absolutely no luck so far! On the contrary; we now have another two broody hens to contend with! I think it must be contagious or something. The other two broody hens are trying to squeeze themselves into one nest box, while 'Houdini' - the only hen who isn't feeling broody - keeps an eye on the food. At least she's got her priorities right!

Oh, and by the way, I'm also growing a forest!

August

Holidays are in full swing. The garden is growing like mad but unfortunately the chickens aren't laying that many eggs.

What more is there to tell?

Writing a blog when 'The Hooligan' was still alive was so much easier and so much fun! She was such a character and got into so much mischief that it was difficult to keep up with it all!

Don't get me wrong, 'Houdini' and 'The Hurkies' are very sweet and cute, but they just don't get up to all that much. As a matter of fact, they might be a bit *too* sweet, if such a thing exists. 'Houdini' is a little bit cheekier than the rest, running up to me every time she sees me, with one of 'The Hurkies', her best pal, following closely at her heels. Do chickens even have heels?

There is still one broody hen who ruffles her feathers every time you try to get her out of the nest box. Once she is out, all she does is a big stinky poo and walks straight back inside again (although as I get ready to send the newsletter, she seems to have come out of her broodiness).

My 'Three Sisters' growing method (corn, runner beans and pumpkin) are growing, but the weather hasn't been all that warm, so the pumpkin isn't doing very much. The runner beans are flowering and the sweet corn is trying to grow too. I'm curious to see if I manage to grow any sweet corn this year.

Once again the greenhouse is infested with aphids. I really am at a loss as what to do next! I've tried spraying the leaves with a soapy solution but I have a bad feeling about this... I may have overdone it. Now the leaves are starting to fall off the plants! If anyone has any ideas or tips, please let me know, I'm at my wits' end and really don't know what to do.

The 'Beechgrove bog' is doing extremely well though and many customers have asked if we have more midges now we have a bog garden and a pond. The answer is that it seems we actually have fewer midges this year. Could it have something to do with the 50 odd tadpoles in the pond? Or do dragonflies eat midges too? I don't know, maybe we've created a good natural balance encouraging plenty of predators with a fondness for midges.

We certainly have lots of bumblebees and bees of various sorts and it's fun to watch them going about their business landing on flowers and gorging on nectar. Sadly, probably because of weather, we've hardly had any butterflies this year. I joined 'The Big Butterfly Count', but only managed to count one small white butterfly in 2 hours! You're only supposed to watch for 15 minutes, but there was nothing to see in that time!

Anyway, we tried our best. You can't change the weather!

The one thing which we are growing lots of is soft fruit, something Scotland is famous for. So far, we've picked 12 kilos (that's 2 stone!) of soft fruit consisting of red currants, strawberries, black currants and raspberries. That's a lot of jam making. A nice job for a rainy day or two. I'm sure there will be many more of those to come!

October

Now, I don't mean to brag... but my potatoes are massive this year! Even if I do say so myself, which I just did!

And the best harvest I've ever had (over 70 kg)!!

The wet weather must have had some positive effect on the growth of potatoes.

Another success story this year has been the soft fruit and the runner beans. We've had 4 times as much soft fruit than last year (red currants, black currants and raspberries) and a massive increase in the runner bean harvest (at least tenfold!) - from a measly 300 grams to well over 3 kilograms! They are native to the rainforest of course, so they don't mind wet, humid weather.

It's been a great September weather wise, with lots of vegetables catching up. We've been harvesting courgettes right up until the end of September and the swallows have been around for at least a week longer than they normally are. I keep a wildlife diary so I know the swallows left around 16th September last year and the year before, but this year I've seen them sitting on the power lines until 26th September. Actually, we had geese and swallows flying over head at the same time! But not together... a sure sign winter is on its way.

You can keep your own wildlife diary at **Nature's Calendar**, details on page 190.

My husband has been building again. We are now the happy owners of, as I like to call it, our very own 'semi-closed veranda'.

It's a very handy place to shelter when it's too windy but still warm enough to sit outside. So now we can enjoy our garden (which is still not quite finished) and stay dry and protected from any strong winds. And if we light a fire pit and some citronella candles, we're protected from the midges too! We've already used it a lot. Of course it will still be too cold in winter to sit there comfortably, but this year it will double as a place to store wood and for drying beans. JP is already planning to build a bigger storage space to house the wood. There's just no stopping him, is there?!

November

'The Hurkies' are normally very well behaved - until a few weeks ago that is. They have now discovered ways out of their (already ample sized) run.

Because we don't want chicken poo everywhere in the garden (and chickens can be pretty destructive creatures too), they are only allowed unrestricted access to the garden once or twice a week, the rest of the time they are kept in a run which not only provides shelter for them but also contains grass and berry bushes. But when JP and I were sitting on the veranda, enjoying the late sunshine one evening we saw 'Houdini' making her bid for freedom from a hole she had found, followed closely by the rest of the escape committee!

So now we have to carefully inspect the enclosure for other means of escape!

We had more excitement the following day, when my hubby cleaned out the henhouse but forgot to leave the hatch open again. So when it got dark, the chickens couldn't get back in!

It was only when JP went to lock them in, he discovered his mistake! But by then, it was pitch black and with the nearest street light miles away, he couldn't see a thing!

We grabbed a torch (with wonky batteries) and went searching for them. Thankfully our chickens are clever little things and we soon found a few perched on top of the wooden fence and the rest hiding in between the gooseberry bushes. So, all were accounted for and we got them safely in for the night and out of reach of 'not-so-fantastic Mr. Fox'.

We've had the first frost in early October when I had to de-ice the car before setting off for work, so the parsnips and kale should be ready. They say that parsnips and kale taste better when there has been a frost - parsnips turn a little sweeter and kale turns softer. I've always been a bit too late to plant out kale for harvesting over winter, but this year I was sure that I had planted them in time. And sure enough... one plant is nice and plump, but the rest are still minuscule. I also sow kale in the greenhouse for harvesting in the 'lean months' between February and April. Normally I sow other leafy vegetables too, but because of family commitments this year we just didn't have enough time to prepare everything. I love my garden but family still comes first.

Never mind, it's a hobby after all and hobbies are meant to be enjoyable!

Did you know...

... that curly kale (or borecole) is very high in **beta carotene**? And it's not even orange!

December

As I write this it's -3°C outside and everything is frozen white (sorry, while checking over the newsletter for the last time, the temperature has dropped to -5°C!). We already had some snow at home in early November and it really feels like winter has now well and truly started (although the meteorological winter doesn't start until the winter solstice on 21st December). It seems I harvested the last remaining parsnips and carrots just in time - the ground is frozen solid now! Sadly most of the parsnips have holes in them - some sort of grub has been munching on them!

Thankfully the carrots have survived intact.

We're now eating kale, sauerkraut and frozen runner beans. There really isn't much left to eat in the garden (except kale and cabbage) and I don't think we'll manage to be self-sufficient for 11 months of the year like we were last year.

With not much to do either, it's time for planning jobs for next year. The bog garden is likely to be extended and we're planning on building a bridge over it. There is a natural, wet area right next to the 'Beechgrove bog garden', so it would only make sense to combine the two.

We'll also be getting a couple of wwoofers again next year. Last year we had to put everything on hold due to family commitments and although we still managed to grow approximately 130 kg (!) of fruit and vegetables; make around 60 jars of jam; 4 jars of chutney and 7 gallons of wine, we couldn't make or grow everything we would have liked to. I know, 7 gallons of wine sounds a lot, but it's not really if you use it for bartering and as Christmas gifts, like we do!

Last but not least; 'Houdini and The Hurkies' (our short legged hens) are still doing their thing. We've fenced off the veranda (if it was up to them, they would sit there all day and poo everywhere!) so now they can go into the rest of the garden and eat their fill of pesky bugs. Actually, they're not even doing that either! Just now all they do is stay in their run or wait underneath the bird feeder! What are they like, eh?! Come on guys, do something.

It'll give me something to write about!

'The Hooligan' hopes you enjoy the gallery of photographs presented on the next few pages, depicting life in and around Glendevon. She strongly feels, however, that she doesn't feature in nearly enough of them!

A dull, uninspired bit of ground when we moved to Glendevon...

...now totally transformed into a productive plot!

Cedric the pheasant hiding from
our chickens!

A spot of gardening with a little help
from my feathered friends.

Robinto flies in for a visit.

Emergency chicken hospital aka our porch!

"Oi! What are you lot lookin' at?!!" enquires Stirling's most famous chicken.

"Feed me Seymour!"
Grow your own monster cabbages...

A hen for all seasons!

...and make them into bucket loads
of sauerkraut!

'The Beechgrove Garden' crew hard at work digging up our garden…

…thankfully not when the garden looked like this, and our local farmer had to dig us out!

The Three Amigas: 'Tufty', 'Caramello' and 'Punky'.

Me as a 1950's housewife in 'Tell it to the Bees'.

One of several guest appearances I made in BBC Scotland's 'River City'.

The ultimate 'staycation' - camping in the tranquility of our own back garden.

Sow an oak...

...or grow your own oats...

...it all benefits wildlife.

Follow the leader! In 'pecking' order... me, 'The Hooligan' and the rest of 'The Chick Peas'.

A Glendevon winter sunset. Good or bad, there's no other place I'd rather to be.

Currants in Black

January

Sigh....! I really wish I had something to tell you this month.

I'm pretty sure you don't want me to start blethering about how many slates we've lost in the recent storms (2), or how many days of snow we've had (1, Boxing Day) or how I managed to get our tiny village Glendevon on the BBC Scotland weather map (I just asked them via Twitter. The weather presenters are really nice folk actually!).

So, instead of boring you with all that, I'll tell you about how our hens are being kept locked in because of the recent outbreak of bird flu.

Some weeks ago the government urged all poultry keepers, big and small, to keep their birds locked in and away from wild birds because of a new strain of bird flu currently gripping Europe.

Last week I read that it had now spread to Scotland. Thankfully we've kept our hens 'in quarantine' for some time.

They don't seem to mind too much. The weather hasn't been that great and they don't wander about much anyway. But to keep them occupied and happy, I've thrown in the left over straw from my threshing experience (imagine what 'The Hooligan', our late foul-mouthed hen, would have said were she still alive!)

Talking of threshing, I finally got around to removing the grains from their husks (or at least tried to!). Since I'm not the owner of a threshing machine I came up with another very useful implement (well two actually) - a rolling pin and an old sheet.

I have to say it was quite fun bashing the stalks and picking out the grains from the sheet, although it did make a bit of a mess of the living room...

All I need to do now is the winnowing (from one bucket to another in windy weather) and milling (grinding two stones together, popular in prehistoric times) to make flour.

And then I'll be able to make my own home grown, home-milled bread or porridge!

February

It's been quite mild for the time of year. Normally January and February are the coldest months of the year, but while I'm writing this (the end of January) it's nearly 10°C! Mind you, we've had some hefty snow showers and hard frosts, so maybe the average January temperature will turn out to be, well, average?!

We've now harvested and eaten all our fresh vegetables from

the garden. There is just overwintering cauliflower (which will hopefully produce a healthy batch of cauliflowers in the Spring), garlic and my wheat, oats and spelt bed, which again should give me plenty of grains this Summer (if only I had found the time to finish winnowing and milling last year's grains! Never mind...).

Oh, and I've got plenty of overwintering kale in the greenhouse, too, which again should start to grow from the end of February onwards when there is sufficient daylight.

Basically, we are only eating beans, pulses and tatties now with pickled vegetables, gherkins and piccalilli.

We've just had to buy carrots and onions so far (we had soft neck rot in our onions, which meant they all spoiled before we could eat them).

If it stays mild we'll be able to 'harvest' and eat weeds sooner rather than later!

I don't know about you, my fellow growers, but my (green) fingers are itching to get started again.

I've already sowed my tomatoes, chillies and aubergines. This year I'm going to try and grow fewer plants. Too many plants can lead to problems with pests in the greenhouse, so my hope is that if I give the plants a long enough growing season, they will produce a larger crop and are less likely to be bothered by bugs.

Some (or maybe all) of the chillies will stay indoors on the windowsill this year. Last year (and the year before) I did grow some chillies, but they never ripened in time. My husband really likes his home made sweet chilli sauce, so I need plenty of the red varieties this year.

Sadly, 'Houdini' and 'The Hurkies' are still locked in their coop because of the recent outbreak of bird flu I mentioned in last month's newsletter. One good thing about this, though, is I can now treat them against worms properly (because the water in their coop is the only thing they have to drink!) and I've been giving them an extra mineral boost in their food, too, which they seem to enjoy!

So much so, in fact, that one of the hens has even started laying eggs again! About time too...

March

I've been patiently waiting for a proper winter to arrive (one with plenty of snow), but so far even where we live (780ft up), we've only had, say, one inch of snow at the very most!

(Update... over 8 inches of snow fell on Thursday 23rd February!)

It's been so mild as well, I think I might have to start mowing the grass again soon!

Global warming, anyone? Although there are still certain influential world leaders who will deny the existence of this...

Anyway, every year at this time I struggle to find something to write about my garden; February is three days shorter and nothing much happens in the garden, everything is still dormant.

But I'm pleased to say that the tomatoes, aubergines and chilli peppers I sowed in January are finally starting to appear. Let the new growing season begin!

I have also planted another crab apple tree. The new plan for the back garden this year is to create various wildlife habitats (for birds, amphibians, insects, butterflies and moths). Each of these will have their own border containing plants appropriate to each species.

For example, the crab apple marks the start of the bird border, which is still covered in black plastic, but as soon as the weather warms up it will be planted out with lots of plants and shrubs that birds particularly love.

The amphibians' border will get an extended bog; a pile of rocks to sunbathe on and they still have the massive pond to breed in, of course.

The butterfly and moth border will feature lots of flowering plants, as well as night flowering plants which tend to suit the moths best. The insect border is an existing wild area, I'll just top it off with a pile of twigs, branches and straw for the little critters to play hide and seek in.

On a different note, my husband and I hope to welcome more wwoofers again this year.

The extra help makes a big difference in what we are able to grow - and is immensely helpful when it comes to making wine and preserves from the fruit etc we collect from the garden.

My husband and I are experienced wwoofers ourselves - we were part of the WWOOF programme when we first came to Scotland 10 years ago, and now we welcome a handful of wwoofers to our place virtually every year. It's a fun way to meet people from all over the world and from different backgrounds and cultures, too.

April

Lots of things have happened in the last month. Some of it good - I've begun sowing again and doing general gardening work. Some of it not so good - 'Houdini' and 'The Hurkies' have been so, so naughty!

Let's start with those misbehaving hens...

JP and I have been away for two weeks visiting friends and family in the Netherlands. I had been telling my parents (also keen 'grow-your-own-ers') that we were looking forward to eating spring cauliflower in just a few weeks time. Before we left, the cauliflowers I sowed had grown into healthy, sturdy plants with small heads forming inside.

But when we got back home.... the vegetable bed had been ransacked. Destroyed. Decimated. You get the idea...

Completely and utterly wrecked! Trashed! By the chickens!

Strangely enough 'Houdini and The Hurkies' mysteriously vanished after I made this shocking discovery. The soup we had that night was delicious, though...

I'm joking of course. We don't kill chickens, not even after they have gorged themselves on our spring vegetables! But to say I was very angry with them is an understatement! Thankfully our neighbour has agreed that we can use a patch of bare land they own, next to our garden, to house the six little cauliflower munching menaces.

And that's exactly where they are now and where they're going to stay. Maybe this year we will be able to create a fenced off area within our own garden for the hens, but we've got so many other projects on the go I'm not sure if we'll have time to fit this in as well. We'll see...

One of the projects we have this year involves replacing more grassy areas (or should I say mossy areas?) with flower borders. We've found it very difficult to grow and maintain a nice lawn in Scotland. The wetter weather and the fact we also have tons of stones in the ground, doesn't help either. We've already built a massive, elevated pond with all the stones and rocks we've dug up and now we're creating a little pond next to it - complete with waterways, more bridges the whole she-bang! Basically, we are extending the 'Beechgrove Garden Bog' to make our garden more adventurous. We'll just have to wait and see how many more midges the extra water attracts.

It's nice that the growing season has started again and to be honest, the weather hasn't been that bad overall. I know we're not out of the woods just yet, but it seems very unlikely we will have snow lying for more than a few days now. Everything is still indoors: I've sowed tomatoes, chillies and aubergines in January and they are coming along nicely. I've also pre-planted onions in the greenhouse and sowed the Dutch 'kapucijner' peas at the start of March. Needless to say the chickens are banned from the greenhouse, so I've still got some kale left to harvest. The weeds have started growing too, so I can always eat ground elder (which is actually quite tasty!), nettles, sorrel and dock leaves.

May

My husband insisted I tell you the story of our neighbours' chicken's quest... to invade and conquer our garden!

So here goes... are you sitting comfortably?

Once upon a time... our neighbours had three lovely hens who liked to roam around our house. But they also liked to jump over our fence into our garden at the back, destroying the pots we've planted bulbs in. They are probably after bugs and beasties, which is fair enough, but does nothing for the appearance of our ornamental pots.

Firstly we lined the pots with chicken wire to keep them out, but then they decided on another course of attack - to sneak into our garden and dig out our newly planted heather plants! Thankfully the heather survived.

Next, my husband covered every single entrance point with more chicken wire, even tying string across the fence to deter them from jumping over it.

It seemed to work for the first few days, but then we woke to the sound of sawing and hammering coming from behind some bushes (Monty Python and the Holy Grail reference, there), only to find out that the resourceful chickens had built a stile to gain access to our garden!

No, not really, but they did manage to break in again... somehow!

My husband is now at his wits' end. I suppose we'll just have to keep on covering any sensitive plants we have and our ornamental pots. Sorry Mrs J (our neighbour), I know there's nothing you can do to stop them either! They're a very determined bunch.

Now for something completely different...

My husband has more projects on the go this year, it really is never ending. One of them is to build a bigger woodshed, the other is to build a small patio for us to sit out in the sunshine and enjoy the peace and quiet!

He had to dig out quite a lot of soil to create a level surface. With us being situated over 700ft up a hill I worried he might hit bedrock and a patio would be out of the question. But when I came home one Saturday afternoon, I discovered he had managed to dig out the main seating area without encountering any massive boulders.

But when he started to create steps leading into the vegetable garden he stumbled across an enormous rock which we estimate weighs approximately 300 kilos! Believe it or not, with the help of our neighbour, he actually managed to lift it out and roll it out of the way. Fun fact: we used to live in Amersfoort, a city also known as 'City of the Boulder Towers'. How ironic!

So, we're planning to eventually make a feature out of this impressive rock - something to add to our ever growing list of things to do! As if we didn't have enough projects on the go!

June

What beautiful, mainly dry weather we've had!

It's around 26°C while I'm writing this and one thing's for sure, the garden absolutely relishes it! Although I prefer it just a wee bit cooler personally...

April has been very, very dry in Glendevon and the reservoirs are way below their normal water levels, which is quite scary. Apparently, (according to one villager who keeps track on precipitation) there was only 6mm rain in the whole of April instead of the usual 100mm. That's down 94%!!

I had just planted some trees and shrubs and they need a lot of water in their first few weeks to establish a good root system, so all my water butts (5 with a capacity of 400 litres each, totalling 2000 litres) were empty within a few weeks. We even had to water the 'Beechgrove Garden Bog' regularly because some plants were looking a bit droopy and sad.

But there are good things that come with having a long spell of dry weather, too; JP finished our patio in one go. Because he had to cement the breeze blocks together (all left over from some building work we had done last year) and then apply something called 'mono couche' (to give them a white finish), we thought it might take the whole summer. Cementing on a dry day, waiting 2 weeks for more dry weather, more cementing, waiting 3 weeks for dry weather etc etc. But of course, he didn't have to wait at all - he managed to finish the whole thing in just 2 weeks!

The warm weather has been great for our fruit trees too. For the first time ALL our apple and pear trees are flowering like mad and they look really beautiful.

I've come to the conclusion that there are 4 stages to successfully growing stone fruit in Scotland:

1. Flowers - if you get a late frost, that's it! **No fruit**
2. Pollination - if it is too cold/wet/windy. **No fruit**
3. Fruit swelling - if it's too cold or too dry. **No (or tiny) fruit**
4. Fruit ripening - if it's too cold/wet/windy. **No ripe fruit**

Basically it means... don't count your chickens* (er, apples!) before they hatch (er, ripen)!

I am slightly worried about the pollination now. Usually this is the perfect weather for bees but since the beekeeper left, we don't have that many bees any more!

I have been using a small paint brush to hand-pollinate, but time will tell whether this is going to be our first year where we are finally able to pick ripe apples and pears!

July

It's been perfect growing weather lately - sunshine, showers, more sunshine, more showers and so on! Quite mild as well and the effect in the garden is noticeable. Everything is growing like their lives depend on it, which from the plant's perspective, I

*Had to have at least one mention of chickens in the newsletter!

suppose it does! And all of a sudden we have plenty of fresh fruit and vegetables from the garden - like endive; all sorts of soft fruit; peas and sugar snaps. We might even be able to harvest some young potatoes later in the month, too.

Did you know that growing soft fruit is really simple? And because soft fruit is so expensive from the supermarkets, it's worthwhile having a go. Basically you buy a plant, say raspberry or red currant, plant it in the garden and just let it do its thing. They'll even grow happily in partial shade! Well, both are native to Northern Europe, so I would expect them to thrive without any help from us!

Stop the press... The chickens are on a diet...

When my husband went to buy more chicken food the other day he complained to the staff that 'Houdini' and the 'Hurkies' weren't eating it and only went for the mixed grain (which is a lot more expensive). The staff were very helpful and said that mixed grain should be something you only give them as a treat and not as their main meal. They said it's like giving children treats all the time and after a while they won't want to return to eating their normal diet. So, our chickens are now on a strict diet of proper layer pellets, which contain all the nutrients they need for laying eggs. Of course, just like children, chickens are not daft enough to starve themselves and so reluctantly they started eating the layer pellets again. It was either that or go hungry! As a result they started laying again and actually look a lot healthier too, although they don't seem very happy about it! By the way, they seem to think the spelt, oat and wheat grain we're growing is for them too!

August

So far this year the flowers have been amazing! Literally everything has - or is in the process of - flowering; my beloved irises (flowering now for the first time since I moved them two years ago); the cherry tree; the fruit bushes; the elder trees are covered in white flower heads and all our ornamental flowers are blooming wonderfully.

Naturally, I thought this would mean we would get lots of fruit too, but that hasn't necessarily been the case. Don't get me wrong, I'm not complaining, we have lots of strawberries, black and red currants and the peas and courgettes are doing reasonably well too.

Carrots, on the other hand, are another story. They are not growing at all!

And I'm not alone either. A lot of other people have said the same thing! It seems that none of the root vegetables are doing very well this year. One of our shop reps - who also grows her own vegetables - was complaining that her parsnips were not germinating (I've had the same problem); one of our regular customers also told me her carrots were not growing much either and even my parents in the Netherlands said their root vegetables haven't been doing very well at all!

I'm now more and more convinced that some years are better than others for growing flowers, some better for roots or leaves or fruits and I'm not 100% sure that weather is the only contributing factor. I get the feeling there might be more going on than we realise...

Ever since we moved into our home seven years ago, we've been converting the garden from a dull, uninspired grassy field into an ornamental garden with an abundance of flowers, trees and shrubs as well as areas where we can just kick back and relax.... not that we have that much *time* to relax in between growing our own vegetables and fruit, of course!

It's still not entirely finished yet, but it's getting there. This is the first year we can sit in the garden and simply enjoy it - without feeling too guilty about not having tackled all of the unfinished areas. Thankfully we've had some really splendid days to do just that!

Sometimes when I look at old pictures, it's hard to imagine that it's the same garden. There is also a lot more wildlife in our garden than there was when we started. We now get lots of birds (including rarer species like nuthatch); there are butterflies, a lot of different moths (I've even spotted a 'garden tiger' moth) and the pond attracts frogs and toads, of course. I don't just do all this gardening for myself, but for nature too. Taking time out to chill and listen to the birds and crickets; watch butterflies weave their way in and out of the flower beds not only gives my husband and I a great deal of pleasure but also fills us with a tremendous sense of achievement!

September

First my exciting non-garden related news.

If you were wondering why I wasn't in the shop for a few days last month, the news is that I have been performing as an 'extra' (or background artist as others prefer to be called!) for a rather modestly budgeted film called 'Tell it to the Bees'. I only signed up with a casting agency six weeks ago, so I was over-the-moon to be selected to star, sorry, appear in this film featuring Anna Paquin, Kate Dickie and Holliday Grainger. It's set in the 1950's and is about an 'unconventional' love affair set in a small Scottish village. I can't say too much about it, but I look very fetching in my 1950's costume and stylish period hairdo!

So far I've filmed for three full (long and exhausting) days and I've participated in a lot of scenes, but you never know which ones will make it to the final cut. I'll just have to be patient and wait and see if my movie debut even makes it to the big screen...

As for the garden, my husband has been at it again. Building, that is. His latest project: a bigger woodshed. Since we rely, almost solely, on a wood burning stove during the winter, we need a lot of wood to keep the house from freezing. So, a bigger wood shed is a necessity. I'm quite happy with it and it looks immaculately clean at the moment - because it's empty. I wonder what it will look like next spring after a few months of storing wood!

My vegetables are looking pretty good. I've grown a monster cabbage - it's massive! I don't know how much it weighs yet and it's still got a long way to go to measure up to the mega sized vegetables people grow for competitions, but it will still make lots of sauerkraut to feed us during the cold winter months, and that's good enough for me!

My tomatoes are also looking pretty succulent. This year has been more successful than previous years and I've also learnt that it's best to grow French beans indoors. The potatoes are slightly smaller than last year, but I'm still pretty confident it will be a good crop.

It's usually when the geese arrive in September that we start to wind down. You harvest, you preserve and you get your wood supply ready. All before winter comes. Then when winter arrives, you can finally relax and reap the benefits of all the hard work you did over the summer.

I have to say I really look forward to the time I can sit back and relax in front of a roaring fire.

That's if I'm not needed on the film set!

We had a lovely wwoofer from New Zealand staying with us mid June and she was shocked by the long days we have in Scotland around this time of year. She even took a picture of the sunshine at 9.45pm and sent it to her family asking what time they thought it was (they all guessed around late afternoon). She also experienced midges for the first time, poor girl. She didn't know what they were until we told her and we were eaten alive the next day while out in the garden. When the midges are really bad, we generally don't go out much in the garden, but we were forced to go out and plant the courgettes!

> With my TV extra work beginning to take off and giving me plenty more to write about, my blog becomes 'Josine's Garden, **TV,** Chicken and Bog Blog' for some considerable time.
>
> Although the 'Bog' part is dropped in the new year!

October

Right, that's the first ground frost been.

Living a little bit more rural (and relatively high up) means you get frost and snow earlier as well as strong winds. But after having lived in Glendevon for nearly seven years, I really should be used to it by now.

My courgettes are nice and cosy, all tucked in under their fleece. They have been all summer really - I only grow hardy vegetables outdoors. My French beans were in the greenhouse, where they gave us quite a good crop this year.

I don't know about fellow home growers, but my courgettes produced masses of fruits, literally kilograms! I normally grow one plant in the greenhouse (you just never know what kind of summer you're gonna get in Scotland) and around three plants on the vegetable plot. All of these have given us lots and lots of courgettes. So I've had to get inventive... making pickled courgette; courgette & runner bean chutney and courgette & other vegetable piccalilli. My mother also makes courgette jam, but I haven't got around to trying that yet!

Other success stories this year have been the cabbages (as mentioned in the last newsletter) which we tried to 'trade' with our neighbours, only to find they also had a bumper crop of cabbages! The runner beans have been doing pretty well too. But my absolute pride and joy is the solitary pumpkin I managed to grow in the greenhouse. I know it doesn't sound like much, but it's such a struggle to grow pumpkins over here that I consider even growing one a major victory!

I haven't been writing much about the hens lately, simply because they haven't been doing anything worth writing about! Sadly, we lost one due to ill health a few weeks ago, so there are now only five hens left.

One of 'The Hurkies' is - how can I put this politely? I can't. She's stupid. I don't understand how she can still function properly because she can't quite seem to grasp the concept of eating! Every time I feed the hens some titbits, she just watches with a 'glaikit' look on her face, while the others scoff them all up. See? How daft is that...?

Winter is quickly approaching and that means it's time to slow down and enjoy a little bit of rest and recreation; maybe do some cross stitching; jigsaw puzzles and hopefully more TV 'extra' work will present itself. If that wasn't enough I'm also starting an Open University access course on science, technology and maths...

November

I can't believe it's the start of November already! Where has the time gone?!

In the garden I'm now preparing the beds for winter, that means adding a layer of compost and cardboard, which rots down over the winter and spring months, adding even more nutrients to the soil.

My studies at the Open University have begun and my first

workbook is about 'life'. It's something I'm interested in greatly: soil, ecosystems, plants, farming, the effect human life has on the planet. I'm learning lots of interesting new things and some things I've already been practising myself - like crop rotation.

Part of this module involves maths, a subject I'm not very confident in and hated at school. Thankfully up until now, we've only covered how to use a calculator! So far, so good.

Anyway, back to the garden...

Officially, 2017 is the year of the monster vegetables!

We've already had the white cabbage which weighed in at a whopping 4kg (all the other cabbages grew bigger than ever before, too)! We are still harvesting the biggest raspberries we've ever had and when it came time to harvest one particular parsnip, I felt like I was on an archaeological dig! It took me 15 minutes to 'excavate' the parsnip before being able to finally pull it out! I've already noticed that the other parsnips are also on the large side and so is the 'Hamburg Parsley' (a root vegetable which tastes like a cross between parsley and a parsnip). The weather apparently wasn't that bad this year after all. If you're a vegetable, that is...

Since the last newsletter, I haven't done much TV and film extra work, just Scottish soap 'River City', which should be broadcast in February. I'm afraid I'm sworn to secrecy (for fear of spoiling any up coming storylines), but I don't think I'm giving too much away when I tell you I'm a 'passer-by' in a few scenes. If you look very closely in the background you might see a blurry figure in a pink jacket, carrying a grey shoulder bag - that's me!

I'm actually wearing my own clothes and carry the same bag I always bring with me to work!

My husband, JP, is also involved in filming as an extra at the moment. The film, called 'Outlaw King', is the story of Robert the Bruce (presumably told Hollywood-style). As he is so tall, he has actually been cast as an English soldier. And despite some pretty poor conditions (mud, rain, getting up at 4am, not getting back home 'til after 8pm poor lunch facilities) he's really been enjoying it! He hopes to get involved in the final battle scenes too (the only thing is; he's supposed to grow a beard, and after nearly 4 weeks he hasn't got much 'face fuzz' to show for it!).

Did you know...

... that Santa Claus as we know him today is derived from the Dutch figure of **'Sinterklaas'** and made famous by the world's most popular brand of Cola?

December

I'm starting this month's newsletter with some very exciting news!

We've got new chickens! Our neighbours who live half a mile up the road from us not only have hens but a cockerel too. They have no neighbours close enough to hear him crow, so they experimented with a broody hen and put some eggs under her.

And it worked... we are now the proud owners of a random mix of cute little chickens.

We have named them 'The Wee Ones' aka 'Punky', 'Tufty',

'Caramello', 'Great White' and 'Small White' and they are absolutely adorable!

Apparently some (or all) are meant to be bantams, which is a small breed of chicken. The cockerel is, however, 'average' sized, so his offspring might turn out to be 'medium' sized too. We're also not sure how many of them are male or female, so we'll just have to wait and see!

The good thing about starting with young chickens is that you can teach them things. They have already passed the first test: eating a variety of different food, which they did with no complaints whatsoever. The last lot were very fussy!

They are, however, still getting to grips with the ramp leading to their night quarters. So far they only want to go in at night when we dangle bits of grass in front of them, although they also went in during the day all by themselves, as if to show me how clever they could be!

'The Wee Ones' have also made friends with a robin, or did the robin make friends with them? Not sure, anyway, this robin is a clever and bold bird; eating the chicken's food and hopping out of the way when one of the more curious chickens comes too close for comfort.

As you can imagine there is not much happening in the garden just now. I've prepared some planters with spring bulbs and cleared the remaining vegetable beds. It is unbelievable how many white cabbages I grew this year, I even brought some into the shop to sell (5 cabbages had a combined weight of 8kg!). They were snapped up!

And I pickled the last of the cabbages with grated beetroot, vinegar, sugar and star anise. It looks really nice, a very bright red colour, but it will be a few months before it'll be ready to eat. As with all pickled vegetables, it tastes better the longer you leave it. More time for the flavours to develop. And besides, I'm still harvesting parsnips, Hamburg parsley (root) and scorzonera. So, no need to start on the stored vegetables just yet.

I don't think I'll be without vegetables this winter... I've pickled 42 large jars of all sorts of veggies and we've got 7kg of sauerkraut to see us through! Pretty sure that's going to be enough... won't it?

2018

When Berry Met Cherry

January

Have you noticed? Winter is well and truly here!

The ground is frozen solid, we've eaten nearly all the fresh vegetables, but at least the house is cosy and warm.

There is very little to do in the garden at the moment, even the left-over root vegetables are stuck in the ground! Our new chickens, 'The Wee Ones' (aka 'Caramello', 'Punky', 'Tufty', 'Great White' and 'Small White') are not that 'wee' any longer, they are growing fast and 'Tufty' is now brave enough to eat out of my hand. Hopefully it won't be too long before they start laying. I really miss my egg at breakfast time!

A lot of people have asked me if you need a large garden to grow your own vegetables and I always say 'no, you can grow some vegetables in a small space too! All you need is careful planning'. The area in which I grow my vegetables is not massive either; around $50\,m^2$ and that seems to be sufficient for me and my hubby, JP. This time of the year is the ideal time to start planning ahead for the new season.

JOSINE ATSMA

Firstly, ask yourself a few questions:

- What do I like to eat? There is no point growing things you don't like!
- How much sunlight does my garden get? Although most vegetables like to have at least a few hours of sun per day, there are vegetables that don't mind shade. If you have a very shady garden, go for lettuces, chard, radishes or cabbages.
- What are the terms & conditions for gardening if I rent my home?
- How much time can I dedicate to gardening?

Once you have considered these questions carefully, it's time to draw up a plan!

This is just one example of a small scale home growing plan, based on roughly 1m² (around 1 foot² per each type of vegetable). I've added a couple of strawberry plants in the schedule, because take it from me - nothing beats the taste of home grown strawberries!

Spring (from April - June)		
Lettuce	Strawberry	Strawberry
Peas (Tom Thumb)	Early radish	Radish
Parsnips	(Empty)	Quick grow swedes

Summer (from June - end September)		
Lettuce	Strawberry	Strawberry
Peas (Tom Thumb)	Runner beans	Cabbages
Parsnips	Carrots	Cabbages

Winter (from end September - January)		
Curly kale	Strawberry	Strawberry
Chard	Late cut & come again lettuce	Cabbages
Parsnips	Carrots	Cabbages

Of course, you can play around with what you want to grow - nothing is set in stone! Just make sure you read the information written on the seed packet - you'll need to familiarise yourself with how big something grows and the individual requirements needed for each plant.

If you are growing on a small area, I would suggest you buy small plants, because it's a lot less time consuming and you don't need to worry about soil temperature too much.

Cabbages take up lots of space, so you can only grow one per square foot. If you feel adventurous you can always make one cabbage into sauerkraut to eat during the winter months, like we do.

I also left out potatoes, onions and garlic. They take up a lot of space and are fairly cheap to buy in the supermarket. But you could plant one clove of (supermarket) garlic in between the other vegetables in November and come October the following year you should have a whole new garlic bulb! Top tip!

So you see... even in a small garden you can still grow a variety of your favourite vegetables.

To be continued in next month's newsletter...

February

It has been confirmed just this morning! 'The Great White' (one of our new chickens) is indeed a cockerel. Last week it made a few pathetic attempts at crowing (not so much cock-a-doodle-do, more cock-a-doodle-don't!), and tried again earlier this week without much success. But the sound it made this morning leaves us in no doubt - it was unmistakeable. This chicken is definitely a cockerel!

He probably surprised himself with the racket he made, not to mention the other four hens!

The slight problem we have, though, is we keep chickens for their eggs and (last time I checked) a cockerel cannot lay eggs! Besides, our neighbours are not too keen on being rudely woken up by him so early in the morning. So, the question is: What do we do now?

He is very timid by nature - nowhere near the top of the pecking order! He is white with a few yellow feathers thrown in. So... if you're interested in giving him a good home, just let me know!*

We are still well and truly in the midst of winter, with the snow only starting to melt today. We've had about 7 - 8 inches of snow the last few days, which makes the garden look like a picture postcard. But of course, there is no gardening just yet, apart from trying to get the last remaining leeks out of the still frozen ground. And the usual planning ahead I do this time of year, of course!

So, as promised last month, here is part two of 'small scale gardening for beginners':

In the last newsletter I set up a growing plan for $1m^2$ growing, but don't despair, if you haven't got a garden or are unable to plant things where you live, because you can also grow a few vegetables in growing bags, pots or even on your windowsill!

Vegetables ideal for deep bags (available from garden centres and Poundstretcher) include potatoes, Jerusalem Artichokes, scorzonera, peas, dwarf French beans and lettuces.

You can plant dwarf varieties of fruit trees in large pots, but make sure you ask the garden centre to confirm it really is a dwarf variety, or you could end up with a fruit tree bursting out of its pot!

What works really well on a windowsill is 'cut-and-come-again' salad leaves. Basically this means that a few weeks after you sow them, you can simply cut off what you need and the leaves

* Sadly 'The Great White' is no longer with us.

should grow back again ready to harvest in another few weeks. This way of growing salad leaves is also good for your pocket, because salad bags are really quite expensive in the supermarket and you can buy seeds for around £1. There are also lots of varieties to choose from: like spicy salad leaves, mild, oriental, single varieties etc.

You don't even have to spend lots of money on pots, you can make them yourself from newspaper (just check online), or use old yogurt pots - in fact any old plastic pot will do as long as you can cut holes in the bottom to let excess water drain out.

If you are growing things in pots or on the windowsill, compost is a must. If you can, try and get peat free compost which is much better for the environment. Or better still get compost from the council, which you can uplift from most recycling centres, just bring along your own bag to put it in. And it's free!

The only thing you have to spend money on is seeds, but even then you can swap seeds with other growers.

I hope I have inspired some of you to grow your own produce, it truly is a rewarding experience. It keeps you fit, provides some much needed vitamin D (in the form of sun light) and gives you delicious, healthy, fresh fruit and veg to enjoy at the end of it!

March

There is still not much to do in the garden at the moment, but I have started sowing sweet peppers and chilli peppers - indoors, of course. I'll probably start to sow tomatoes later in March,

126

once again in the greenhouse.

In the previous two newsletters I hopefully inspired some of you to grow your own vegetables.

This might not be for everyone, but you could always create a garden which is beneficial for wildlife if you prefer.

One of the things you might like to do, with the kids for example, is to build your own wildlife pond.

I'm not talking about digging a massive hole in the garden and filling it with water, although feel free to do that if your garden's big enough! Why not start off with an old tub, large tray or washing up basin and fill it with rain water?

In my previous garden, I used an old washing machine drip tray to create a water feature in a corner of the garden. I added a few water plants and placed plant pots and rocks all around it and it looked great!

Water is just so important for wildlife - you can't really go wrong with it. Even a small size water feature will attract all sorts of creatures. Birds might use it to bathe in and drink from, dragonflies might drop by and land on the plants and if it's slightly bigger, frogs or toads might spawn in it!

Just make sure you incorporate a slate or a large branch to act as a ramp, so animals can get out if they accidentally fall in!

Sadly, we no longer have a cockerel; it's just the four girls left now. Strangely enough they are less skittish now that the cockerel has gone. He would correct them when they strayed and had started making, er, unwelcome advances towards them. I think they were slightly intimidated by him, which in turn made the hens more wary of JP and I - running off any time we approached them.

I think I have to rename the hens though, because they now look more like members of a rock band! There are the two with punk hairdos ('Punky' and 'Tufty') and then there is 'Caramello' - she's got a couple of black feathers in her tail and now looks like a combination of Vyvyan and Rick from the '80s comedy show 'The Young Ones'!

So, perhaps I should name them the 'Glendevon Rockers' or the 'S-eggs Pistols'!

I don't think it'll be too long now before they start laying eggs. 'Caramello' has found a spot in the garden where she likes to just sit and generally speaking they seem more relaxed and less timid. I don't want them to be too clingy though: cute as it is having hens follow you around the garden, it's not very handy when you have work to do!

The TV and film industry is coming out of hibernation and when this newsletter goes out, I'll already have returned to Shieldinch, the fictional Glaswegian district featured in BBC's 'River City'. When I first registered with the casting agency, I imagined myself sitting inside 'The Tall Ship' (the River City pub), chatting over a glass of fake red wine. And that's exactly what I did last week!

Filming took place entirely in a studio this time and looked so real that every time the pub door opened I kept expecting to feel a draught!

Oh by the way, I appeared in two scenes in the episode broadcast on Tuesday 20th February - did you manage to spot me?

I'm still hoping I get selected for the TV show 'Outlander' though - that would be my dream come true! Unfortunately it's every other extra's dream job too! Recently I was very close to being selected and although my agent did his best to try and squeeze me in they were just too full. Part of the attraction for me is the dressing up in historical costume - can't think of anything better than slipping into a dress from the 18th century and playing make believe!

I'll keep you updated on my experiences!

April

Well, well, well... what can I say? We had so much snow last month!! Not just up here, everywhere down there too! Because my husband and I live half a mile off the main road, we were snowed in for nearly five days - the local farmer had to finally dig us out with his tractor!

Thankfully, all the snow has melted and I can finally look forward to the new growing year. We will be welcoming our first wwoofers at the end of March. Hopefully we can get the vegetable beds ready and the wood shed stocked up. When you've solely been eating seasonal winter vegetables for what seems like forever, you really look forward to 'green food' like salad leaves again. Normally I would now be eating nettle soup, various 'weeds' from the garden and sorrel, but because of all that snow, hardly any shoots have appeared just yet.

Now, I've got an equation for you to ponder:

1 robinto + 2 robinta = **lots of robintii**

No idea what I'm blethering about?? I'm not too sure myself! But let me try and enlighten you...

Every morning during the winter months, we've been feeding tasty morsels to a very cheeky robin. He is pretty tame now and even eats from JP's hand every once in a while! He waits patiently for us when we let the hens out, because that's when he gets fed. He has been entertaining us with his birdsong for the last few weeks and he's also managed to charm not one, but two female robins. We've named him 'Robinto' and are now calling the girls 'Robinta'. Of course, as you know, when a girl bird and a boy bird love each other very much... you can expect to get lots of chicks, or 'robintii' as we like to call them!

As for the TV extra work, I've recently been involved in filming scenes for a new BBC drama. I don't really know anything about it yet - I met some really nice people, but the whole experience wasn't as much fun as I thought it would be this time round. A *lot* of hanging around...

JP has also featured as an extra in 'River City' and was filmed sitting in the exact same spot in the 'pub' as I was! What a coincidence - feels like I was just keeping the seat warm for him! By the way, being an extra doesn't guarantee you will necessarily be seen on TV. Of course, sometimes you ARE seen - sometimes more than once! I was seen twice in the latest episode to be broadcast. Jammy or what?

May

What a peculiar month April has been! Easter fell very early this year, resulting in very cold weather and for some of us (including me and JP) yet more snow! We had some 8 inches of snow lying from Easter Monday until Wednesday. You think we'd be fed up with it by now! Maybe a little bit...

I felt sorry for our poor French wwoofers, but they had been volunteering all winter in the UK and had become quite accustomed to the colder weather. Of course we couldn't do much in the garden, so they cleared out the greenhouse, which was brilliant! Another job we were glad to have an extra pair of hands with was moving a small greenhouse across the road to our neighbours. Because we are a bit more exposed, we had to place the greenhouse next to our house, which meant it didn't get any sun. So, our neighbours had a much better spot for it, and we offered it to them, so that's where it ended up. We built an outdoor run for the chickens at the side of our house (in the site vacated by the greenhouse) which actually turned out really well! I planted it with 'chicken friendly plants', or should I say: 'plants chickens really like to eat'?!

Unfortunately the hens are not really enjoying their new run, because the plants have to establish themselves first, before they have the chance to destroy them. They are, however, enjoying making a racket outside our garden! As we live pretty remotely (away from any busy roads) we just let the hens run around wherever they want... the front path, the road, the fields, the neighbours' garden...

Because of the long, long winter our garden is a little behind with everything. Our first frog spawn appeared the second week in April; our daffodils are just beginning to flower now in the last week of April; our helleborus plants are still fully flowering but I haven't planted much in the vegetable beds just yet. I had to pre-sprout the onion sets, because we couldn't plant them sooner. Anyway, normally everything catches up as soon as the weather warms up a bit, so I'm not overly worried just yet...

I had some fantastic news the other week - the 'Bumblebee Conservation Trust' confirmed that we are the proud 'owners' of the rare 'Bilberry Bumblebee' after spotting one in the garden! Planting all those wildlife friendly plants and shrubs has paid off it seems, which I'm over the moon about.

As of mid April I'm back doing some TV extra work again. Keep an eye out for a birthday party scene in 'River City' to be broadcast in the summer. I was selected to be one of the main characters' 'friends'. I don't have any lines (extras don't say anything!), but I can be seen mingling with the main actors as well as the other extras. By the way, most of the other extras I've met are very experienced with the majority of them having between 10 and 15 years experience of doing extra work! I've only been doing this since July last year!

Sorry to those who follow 'River City', but I can't say anything more about the scene, except that it was filmed in one of the studio 'living rooms' and it gets quite intense! I had another TV extra job this month, too - but it wasn't all that exciting after all

- I was in a group of six and none of us were even used. We just hung around until we were released five hours later, which felt like an eternity! A complete waste of a day... just think what I could have accomplished in the garden in that time!

June

I've been living in Scotland for so long now that I blend in with the locals when it comes to skin tone. When I was over in the Netherlands at the end of May, my very pale skin made me stick out like a sore thumb - everyone else seemed so sun tanned! Thankfully the weather has turned sunny and warm and I'm slowly beginning to catch up now.

So is the garden by the way. All our fruit trees are flowering like mad, the soft fruit bushes are laden with currants and everything in general is back on schedule.

The nice weather also meant I could finish landscaping the garden. Our final borders have been dug and planted and now it's just a matter of keeping on top of the weeds and perhaps moving a few plants to a better location.

Change of plans again though... the original 'Five Senses' garden (as I explained on 'The Beechgrove Garden' some years ago now) has been made into a butterfly and moth border brimming with lots of flowering plants butterflies just love.

The 'Five Senses' part of the garden has now moved closer to the house. I have four small boxes with plants for each sense, while the fifth sense 'hearing' is represented by the entire garden. You'd be surprised how much noise nature makes! What a racket! All I have to do now is make signs for each bed: 'taste me', 'smell me', 'touch me', 'see me' and 'hear me' which I will attach to the veranda.

I now finally have my own herb garden! It's divided into four sections; 'colds & flu', 'digestion', 'sleeping' and 'legends'. It contains herbs which I also sell in the shop, so now I can make my own decoctions for the very few times I feel a wee bit under the weather (although I hardly ever catch anything!). Anyway, it's nice to be able to dry herbs like elderberries, sage, thyme, meadow sweet and more for the colder months just around the corner.

The chickens are also doing well. 'Punky' seems to think she's broody, but she won't make a good mother because she perches at night, leaving the imaginary eggs in the cold. After she has been sitting on her 'eggs' for an hour or so she just walks off and abandons them so she can join the rest of the gang. But when she is sitting in the nest and you look at her, she puffs herself out and makes an awful screeching noise, which is really quite unsettling, to be honest! Even the neighbours were asking if she was feeling alright!

On the film & TV extra front... it'd probably be a lot easier if 'River City' just added me to their payroll! I was back in Shieldinch again in May and a couple of days after that they called to say they wanted me back again! Unfortunately the second time was on a Saturday, which is not the best of days for me so I couldn't make it. After all, I still have a shop to run! They are on a summer break so no more filming for 'River City' just now - but maybe I'll be put forward for other TV work or a Hollywood blockbuster, who knows? I'll keep you posted...

July

Keeping chickens is not always as straightforward as it seems. Most of the time it's just a matter of opening the henhouse in the morning, feeding them and locking them in again at night. But occasionally one of them falls ill, or in this case, succumbs to something called 'wry neck'.

It's not really a disease, more like a deficiency or genetic disorder, but it looks really horrible!

The hen's neck becomes crooked, making eating and drinking very difficult. Apparently it's not painful, but it can last for weeks. Of course we are trying to treat 'Tufty' the hen with vitamins and syringe feed her, but it is now been going on for over a week and let me tell you, it doesn't look very nice! She has become pretty attached to us - waiting for me to give her the special bread mix and extra water with vitamins I've prepared for her. At night she waits near the ramp for my husband to lift her up into the henhouse.

She is a 'Silkie' breed and they are more prone to wry neck, we found out that the cockerel (possibly the father) had this condition too. I was hoping that it would clear up over time...

... but sadly a short while before finishing this newsletter, she had another really bad fit which lasted for 20 minutes and it seemed the kindest course of action was just to end her suffering.

The garden is flourishing with lots of fruit forming and, hopefully, ripening as well. We have started harvesting the honeyberries, which are edible honey suckle berries which grow really well in Scotland. If you have space, it might be an idea to get yourself a bush.

Just make sure it says edible on the label!

My strawberries are also ripening and I've harvested my first chard. Despite the storm we had in May, the fruit trees still have most of their fruit and thankfully we escaped the massive hail stones that fell recently, just 6 miles from us! I do like my weather, as all of you know, and of course I was once again mesmerized by these extreme showers, silly isn't it?!

Anyway, for my new studies (I am going to study natural science at the Open University) I get to study some meteorology as well, which is right up my street! I can't wait to start, but first I need to wait for my results from the access course I've already completed.

The next episode of 'River City' airs on 3rd July and I think I might be in that one, as a guest at a birthday party - so keep your eyes peeled! Just as I was putting this newsletter 'to bed', I had just finished filming again for a BBC series, this time as a politician, the second time I've been booked as one. Do I really have the look of a politician about me?! Talk about type casting...

Anyway, being an extra (or 'Supporting Artist' I should say) is really strange. Yesterday we were filming on the streets of Edinburgh and it suddenly struck me: because passers-by have no idea what's going on it feels like the outside world (the 'real world') is somehow a different world, as if there is an invisible line between 'the set' and the 'normal world'. Once I'm back behind the wheel of the car driving home, I revert back and become part of the 'normal world' again. I might be the only one who experiences it like that, but it feels very strange. Weird, huh?

Did you know...

..... the inside of a cucumber can be up to **10°C cooler** than the outside air temperature?

August

Let's start with the big news first: 'Tufty', our poorly hen is still with us!! And I don't mean back from the dead - not a zombie chicken or anything like that. Let me explain...

When I sent last month's newsletter out on the Saturday, we let her out for a final day in the fields, thinking if - by some miracle - she did manage to make it through the day we would still have to end her suffering on the Sunday. When we came home that night, there was no sign of her - she had simply vanished. So, we assumed she hadn't made it and had wandered off somewhere and passed away peacefully. That is until the neighbour came to our door to say she was creating havoc in their garden! We were gobsmacked! My husband went to pick her up and when we examined her, there hardly seemed to be anything wrong with her neck at all! It's still ever so slightly bent over, but nothing like it was weeks ago or even the previous day! We couldn't believe it! Now that she seems to be back to her normal (sweet) self - she's back outside with the rest of the flock again creating chaos in our garden. Apparently the vitamins we gave her had a positive effect and we've continued feeding her the special mash once a week, just to be on the safe side.

They never fail to surprise you, don't they?!

So does the Scottish weather by the way... what is happening to the climate?? It has been incredibly dry and really warm too; by Scottish standards. One of the many reasons I moved to Scotland, is the slightly cooler climate, I don't really like anything over 23°C, but this year there have been plenty of times when temperatures have risen above that. Mind you, in the Netherlands it's currently over 30°C, so it's still a lot cooler over here. But for the first time our garden is not four weeks behind everywhere else! In contrast - because of the extremely hot weather in Holland - my parents' strawberries are behind ours. Not that it's a competition or anything! But what a harvest we've had so far: the strawberries never seem to stop (11kg); the cherries are the best we've ever had (7kg); the onions are so big, they are ready to lift now (something we don't normally do until the end of August) and it looks like we'll be making sauerkraut by the end of August too, instead of September which is the norm!

You normally start storing vegetables from the end of September, which ideally should last you until February or March. But because we've had to harvest everything before September, we might not have enough stored vegetables by the time March comes round! I hope to overcome this by sowing lots of greens (like kale, purslane and endive) in the greenhouse over the winter which should be ready in March or April and help see us through. If I do end up with a glut of something, I will sell it in the shop. The hot weather is also a cause for concern - we can manage to water our garden with watering cans, but large farms can't, so reading how the drought is affecting farmers in the news is commonplace and frightening.

Oh, by the way, did you see 'River City' on 11th July? Or were you watching the footie? Anyway, if you did tune into the best (and let's face it only) Scottish soap, you couldn't have missed me. I was a guest at the Murdoch's birthday party and feature in a couple of key scenes. You can even hear me converse in the background! It's still available to watch at BBC iPlayer, and the party scene is featured around the 20 minute mark. Fame (of sorts) at last!

September

I don't think I've ever come across a hen quite as dumb as our hen 'Punky'!! I mean, honestly, she must've been right at the very back of the queue when they were handing out brains!! For example, when I come home at night the hens all recognise me and come running up to me and I give them some treats. It's our wee daily routine. All the hens except 'Punky' who stays behind, looking around her with a blank expression on her face. It takes a while for the penny to drop that the rest of the flock is no longer there and she starts to panic a little, calling for her friends, who are too busy tucking into their treats to pay her any attention. By the time she has joined them all the treats have gone. Naturally, I feel a little sorry for her, so I eventually slip her some wheat and corn when the others aren't looking.

Thankfully, all is well again with our flock of four hens: 'Caramello', 'Punky', 'Tufty' and 'Mrs. Feathers' (the latter named by Stuart's youngest daughter, Ruth).

I wasn't joking last month when I predicted I'd be making sauerkraut in August; it's already in the big crock fermenting away! Because of the very warm May and June and wetter, but mild, July and August, the vegetables are just growing and growing and growing... We harvested an incredible 12 kg of white cabbages to make sauerkraut and kimchi with. But we still have four large cabbages on the plot. The carrots are also doing really well and this year is the first year I've managed to grow decent sized beetroot! It must be down to our exposed location, but beetroot has never done well with us - but not this year! I've even managed to grow a fancy variety of beetroot with stripes this year, called 'Chioggia'. I'm all chuffed with myself.

The onions are enormous too. I had to start harvesting in order to prevent them from rotting, but now I need a few sunny days for them to dry before storing them for the winter. I don't think I've ever grown vegetables as big as these before, it's astonishing what a slight rise in temperature can do, isn't it?!

As far as the TV extra work goes, it isn't! Not much is being filmed right now - all the other extras (including myself) are just twiddling our thumbs which means when an opportunity does arise, hundreds of extras apply for the same job!

But the trailer for 'Outlaw King' is out now, a film about Robert the Bruce due for release in November. My husband features in it as one of the many soldiers (playing both an English and a Scottish soldier, but not at the same time!). The movie I was an extra in this time last year, 'Tell it to the Bees', is to feature at the Toronto International Film Festival soon. No sign of a trailer for that one yet!

October

We are now heading towards that time of year again where everything starts to wind down. The leaves are turning red, yellow and brown; the robin is singing its wee heart out; the swallows have disappeared and the geese have returned back home.

In the garden it means lifting the last potatoes, protecting tender plants and preserving (or eating) the last tomatoes and cucumbers. But looking back - what a terrific year we've had!

In all honesty, we have never had so much fruit and vegetables! Although the potatoes are smaller this year, the cabbages, carrots, onions and parsnips are gigantic! Good job we had two Italian wwoofers helping out the last two weeks because cutting up 7.5 kg (16.5 pounds) of onions would take a single person a long time... and a lot of tears to be shed! But the wwoofers hardly shed a single teardrop - mainly because they were wearing safety goggles! My top gardening tip this month - always were protective glasses when slicing large quantities of onions!

'Tufty' and her clan are still healthy and thankfully the crooked neck she had seems to have completely healed. Soon, they will be able to eat the pests and bugs in the garden, but for now they are out in the fields (and the neighbours' garden apparently) - up to no good, knowing them!

They shouldn't have any problems finding some insects because, as you know, I grow everything organically and that means I never use any pesticides.

This year I finally created my herb garden and it has been a huge success, too! Some plants are so big (like the borage) that they block the garden path and I have to walk around them to get from one end of the garden to the other.

The bird border which I created last year has exceeded my expectations too. I've planted all sorts of plants and shrubs beneficial to birds: like cotoneaster, sunflowers, juniper shrubs, a crab apple tree and berberis.

We didn't have long to wait before the birds 'flocked' to our garden - we've already counted an impressive 23 different species of birds. We've spotted some rarer species too - like willow warbler, reed bunting and nuthatch. I have to admit, I'm pretty pleased with how it's all turned out!

It just goes to show how important it is to garden without the use of chemicals, you'll be rewarded with lots of different varieties of birds to look and marvel at!

Did you know...

... Halloween comes from '**All Hollows Eve**', thought to have been a special celebration by Irish and Scottish Celts to mark the end of Summer.

November

My husband and I never switch off from living a self-sufficient lifestyle, not even when we go on holiday! We went camping in the south of Germany last month and the camp site we stayed at had lots of apple trees. No one was picking them, so we asked the owner if we could pick the apples and he said sure, pick as many as you like (but in German). So we did! We snacked on them; used them to make apple pancakes and I even used them to make apple puree to have with breakfast!

It seemed such a waste just to let them rot in the ground.

By the way, last time I checked, my husband and I have grown over 200 kilograms of fruit and vegetables this year! Impressive.

We had a lovely holiday travelling, meeting family and friends, but when we came home we noticed one of our hens, 'Mrs Feathers', had a limp wing. At first we thought it might just be sprained but when she showed no improvement after four days, I examined her more closely and I now suspect she has broken it. There is not much you can do about a broken wing, apart from strapping it against her body, so that it can heal. When we had the ex-battery chickens, I had little knitted chicken jumpers made to keep them warm if they ever lost their feathers. These fit snugly around a chicken, with a hole for its head and space for the wings, but if you fold it in half, the knitted bit fits around the wings so it offers some support. So, that's exactly what we did! We now have one white chicken with a snazzy pink jumper running around the place!

We also noticed that 'Tufty' had lost all her breast feathers. Apparently some hens peck at their chest feathers when they feel broody, so she also now sports a funky little knitted jumper to keep her warm. They've started a bit of a fashion trend - our neighbours' chickens are so jealous!

By the way, our little, 'tame' robin we fed every morning last winter is back this year again! Great news! He (or she) can be assured there will be some tasty titbits left every morning on top of the chickens' food storage bins. It's just such a nice way to start the day, watching the wee fella tuck into his breakfast treats!

It's been very quiet on the TV extra front lately, I haven't had much free time and there simply isn't that much being filmed requiring extras. But if you have been watching BBC1's 'The Cry' (like 5.7 million other people), you might have spotted a familiar looking face in the background. In episode 3 the main character is sitting in a bar in Australia (actually filmed in Scotland!) and throughout the entire scene you can see me chatting away in the background. This scene is a perfect example of how you just never know whether you will appear on TV or not. There were around 20 other extras on the day, but only three (including myself) appeared in the final shot! I was one of the lucky ones this time, I guess.

December

Unfortunately I'm starting this section of the newsletter with some more sad news. 'Mrs Feathers'- who had what we assumed was a broken wing last month - took a turn for the worse a few weeks back and it was only humane to let her go.

We tried everything we could to save her: we isolated her from the others so we could administer extra vitamins and minerals and give her extra protein. We also tried every possible way to keep her upright, as her balance was severely affected by her illness. But in the end, although she was still eating, she had lost nearly all of her feathers and she couldn't even sit up any longer, let alone walk. As a result she had soiled herself quite badly. At this point we realised it would be cruel to let her go on like this. We expected her condition to improve after a few days of extra vitamins and protein, but her condition actually deteriorated. We think she may have had a stroke or contracted 'Marek's disease', a very contagious viral infection. All the other hens are fine and we have informed our neighbours as well. All we can do is hope it doesn't spread and continue to give the healthy hens extra vitamins, Echinaforce (the echinacea tincture from A Vogel) and keep our fingers crossed.

I haven't been doing any TV extra work for the last couple of months, too busy with my Open University studies (and running the shop!), but my husband can be seen (twice, briefly) in Netflix's epic 'Outlaw King' as both an English soldier (watching Stirling Castle being blown to pieces) and as a soldier fighting for the

Scottish. The reason he was cast twice is because the filming days were so gruelling that they needed all the extras they could get for the battle scenes. We had to pause the film several times so we could pick out JP from all the other soldiers, which was fun. By the way, anyone who is following 'Clique' Series 2 on BBC3 (iPlayer) might have spotted me in the episode broadcast on Friday 30th November. I appear as a very well groomed politician! I know, another one! What's that all about?

Obviously there is not much to tell about the garden at this time of year, everything is pretty much asleep. We are still harvesting from our vegetable beds though - there are still some carrots, parsnips, Hamburg Parsley roots, kale and winter cabbages left. So thankfully we're not down to pickled and fermented vegetables just yet! For the past year (and certainly throughout the whole of this year) we have been self-sufficient in vegetables - except for onions, which just don't store that long. We normally run out of potatoes in April or May too, but then we eat pasta instead. It all depends on how well the roots will store but as my last blog of the year comes to an end, our larder is pretty well stocked and that's a good sign!

2019

Some Like it Hotter

January

I was worried that after the illness of 'Mrs Feathers', our late white hen, the other hens would fall sick too. I'm glad to report that our three remaining hens are alive and kicking! 'Tufty' was going through a moult, but she has grown back a new set of feathers and all of the chickens have started laying again. Although normally hens stop laying during winter time, ours are still going strong - although they do take a day off every now and then, which I guess they are entitled to and is fine by me.

We also had our first winter weather of the season mid-December - freezing rain. This is fairly rare in Britain, it's different from black ice which is basically rain water freezing on the surface of the roads. Freezing rain is supercooled rain which freezes immediately upon contact with any surface. So, it's not just the roads that become icy, but everything else too! I had to close the shop an hour early that day as our main road (A823) became more like an ice rink and our path leading up to the house had more ice than a bob sleigh track! Good job I left early, because when I came home the trees were so heavy with ice, they hang over and touched the roof of the car as I drove underneath them! When I got out of the car, I noticed that a thin layer of ice had also covered the door handle! Plus, I had to give the latch of the gate a hard knock to break the ice off before I could enter the front garden.

I recently joined a vegetable growers group on Facebook and they were complaining about how their parsnips didn't germinate at all this year. Someone posted a picture of her one and only parsnip this year and someone else commented that it was one more than she had managed to grow! Not to brag, but I have lots of parsnips this year and corkers at that, too! One of the reasons for this may be because England had a much longer, drier and hotter summer than we had in Scotland. The parsnips grown south of the border didn't do as well as the ones grown up north. So, you see, sometimes living in a slightly cooler climate can actually be beneficial. Particularly if you like parsnips!

February

What does one write about in the middle of winter? Well, I should know because I do it every year!

It usually goes something like this...

I don't have any exciting snow or ice stories (just yet); the winter so far has been fairly dry and today in Stirling I think the temperature even reached double figures! Even the chickens have been behaving themselves and are very healthy, thankfully - so not much to write about there either! There was one funny thing that happened involving the chickens, though. Our neighbours have just the one white hen left now which feels lonely during the day and joins our three to scratch for worms and insects, as you do. Now that the majority of our vegetables have been harvested, the chickens have free run of the back garden instead of being limited to the fields around us, helping us to get rid of all the nasty little grubs we don't want. The neighbours' hen however is more interested in the bird food scattered on the ground underneath the bird feeder than anything else. Now she seems to have persuaded our hens to look for food there too! Well, at least I don't need to worry about any spilled wheat germinating, I suppose. At the end of an exciting day our hens go back to their night quarters, bidding farewell to the white one. Ours go to bed much earlier than the neighbours' hen, so she patiently waits outside the coop for a while, looking lost, before turning round and trudging back home all on her own. Bit sad really, isn't it?!

Speaking of birds, do you remember last year I told you about the little robin we regularly fed at his or her special table? This year we also have another robin in the front garden with a distinct marking on his or her chest (and I don't just mean a red breast!). We decided to name this robin 'Spot' because of this. Robins are notoriously territorial and 'Spot' has claimed the front garden as his or her own because that just happens to be where the bird feeder is. Not daft, eh? The other day though, another robin with no markings appeared in the garden, so I thought, uh-oh, it had either driven 'Spot' away or 'Spot' might have succumbed to the cold after all. But I was wrong; 'Spot' saw the intruder, chased it away and is now back again defending the bird feeder. Sometimes it's like watching an episode of BBC's 'Winterwatch' through our kitchen window!

I have always been very interested in what happens when you leave nature to do its own thing with no interference from humans. So, a few years ago I decided to leave an area in the back garden roughly 2m² to its own devices and see what happened. I started by sowing a handful of wild flower seeds and the only other thing I do is, once in spring is to clear away the moss. It's remarkable how quickly plants colonise a wild area. Last summer I discovered two tree saplings, one a pine of some sort and the other one, I think, a sycamore. It will be interesting to see if these two trees will survive the winter and continue to grow into adult trees. Although that won't happen any time soon, so I'll just have to be very, very patient. Don't worry, though, I'll keep you up-to-date on any other plants colonising this wild, untouched area.

March

It's amazing (not to mention shocking) how some world leaders still choose to believe there's no such thing as climate change! Here in Scotland we've had the driest January since records began (in this area) and the warmest temperatures ever recorded in February! While on the other side of the pond (not our pond in the garden, the Atlantic Ocean!) Las Vegas has been experiencing both snowfall and just a few days later the hottest temperatures ever! Bonkers!

The weather definitely is changing, how much is down to natural processes and how much is caused by us humans, is another debate entirely!

Anyway, the effects of this warm winter are certainly visible in the garden. I have planted out my young cauliflower plants, (still covered because you just never know!); the birds are singing; the crocuses are flowering and I have even sat outside enjoying the sunshine (instead of studying - I just can't find much enthusiasm for wavelengths and mathematics at the moment). I've also noticed that the coltsfoot is flowering a month earlier than it did last year. 'Nature's Calendar' is an online recording system set up by 'The Woodland Trust', which asks members of the public to keep track of and record certain events in nature - like the coltsfoot first flowering or the first cuckoo heard or seen. Biologists and ecologists use this information to see how weather is affecting wildlife. I have been doing this for a few years now and it is really cool to observe and record the differences myself. So now I know that in my garden not only has the coltsfoot flowered over a month earlier than last year, but our 'resident' cuckoo has been visiting us the exact same week every year! For a couple of years I'm sure it's even been on exactly the same date! 'Nature's Calendar' is free and easy to use and I would recommend giving it a go, if not to help research, then just for the sheer fun of it.

March will also be the month when I start sowing cabbages and tomatoes again and if the weather stays like this, I might even start planting the onions out in the garden. I have already started off my sweet peppers and chilli peppers and they are growing nicely. Because they need such a long growing season it's better to sow them in January indoors on the windowsill and then plant them out in the greenhouse when they get too big.

April

What does one write about when the stars of the show have not been doing anything worth writing about? You find another star, that's what! So, let me introduce you to 'Cedric', our resident pheasant (named by one of our regular customers). He has been strutting around the place for months (the pheasant not the customer) and it always brings a smile to my face when he makes an appearance. Recently he has been making these funny noises (which reminds me of cars skidding round a bend) to attract the ladies. And attract the ladies he has! A few weeks ago, on my way to work, he crossed our path with four female admirers in tow! Either (by pheasant standards) he's a bit of a catch or he's the *only* male pheasant in the neighbourhood!

This time of year always makes me feel happy, uplifted, positive. Flowers are appearing left, right and centre; temperatures are on the up; I've started sowing again and the birds are singing and building their nests. Speaking of birds nesting; I have recently installed a very unusual looking bird box, which resembles an old teapot hung upside down! That's because it is an old teapot hung upside down! I got the idea from a book I was reading and thought, hey, I can do that! So, after rummaging in a charity shop, I found an old teapot, stuffed some wood shavings up the spout and now it's hanging in the garden - ready for the first birds to move in, which I hope will be any day soon. Apparently you can also use old wellies, boots and shoes as bird boxes, too!

By the way, remember the TV and Film extra work I did in 2017 and 2018? Well, one of the films, shot in Deanston way back in 2017, 'Tell it to the Bees', has finally released a trailer and I was totally gobsmacked when I recognised a very familiar face in it. Mine! How cool is that? You can see me off to the side, gossiping about Holiday Grainger, the lead actress, drawing her a really dirty look. I look very different though, with my 1950's hair-do and wardrobe, but my height is a dead giveaway! The funny thing is, this particular scene was actually my very, very first day as an extra. I hadn't done anything along those lines before, while all the other extras on the shoot had done loads of things, so I felt like a right newbie!

I am so excited! I just can't wait for the film to come out! If we are lucky it may be screened in the Macrobert Arts Centre and who knows? I might even make it into the finished film, so keep your eyes peeled for a tall, blonde, 1950's housewife with curly blonde hair. And no, it's not a wig!

May

I could start writing the storyline for a soap opera with our hens, the neighbours' hens and 'Cedric' in the lead roles! 'East-henders', maybe?

Last month I introduced newsletter readers to 'Cedric', a

male pheasant who has been wandering around our place for some months. He is a busy chap; keeping four lady pheasants entertained while patrolling 'his' neighbourhood. Or so I thought! Our hens recognise our car as it pulls up to the house; and knowing that I will feed them some corn, they wait patiently on the drive to greet me. So, when I came home the other day, I saw one of our hens and the neighbours' last remaining one running on the path towards the car. I thought to myself. "That's clever, our hens have told the neighbours' hen about the free corn". How wrong could I be! They weren't greeting me; they were ganging up to chase poor 'Cedric' away! And it gets even worse... the other two, slightly more timid hens, were following behind just to make sure 'Cedric' got off 'their' patch! Chickens are a bit like 'Jekyll and Hyde'; they can be very endearing one minute, then nothing short of pure evil the next!

The new growing season is now well and truly under way; I've sown most of the vegetables and planted out quite a few too. So, we now have tomato plants, sweet pepper plants, peas, onions and potatoes alongside tiny red and white cabbage plants, which will hopefully provide us with enough cabbage to make sauerkraut again for next year. As you know by now, we Dutch love our sauerkraut! This month we only just finished eating the sauerkraut we made last October! Sauerkraut - because it is naturally acidic - keeps for a very long time and that is where our ancestors got their vitamin C from in the 'hungry gap', which traditionally runs from late February until early May. This is the time in the growing season when you have eaten all the winter vegetables, but the new spring vegetables aren't quite ready to consume yet.

Because we had such an incredible season last summer, we still have some carrots left over from last year; there is (overwintered) kale in the greenhouse, pickled vegetables and hopefully the overwintered cauliflower will have formed heads soon too, so no 'hungry gap' for us this year. Even if there was, we can always make the short trip to the supermarket and get our veggies there! Our ancestors didn't have this luxury - how times have changed!

What cracking Easter weather we've had! I managed to start planting and sowing outside, which might be too early, but sometimes you just have to take the chance and go with your gut instinct. The warm weather has also brought out lots of butterflies, bumblebees and bees; I've got 'peacocks', 'small tortoise shells', 'orange tips' and I am also proud to be the 'host garden' of the rare beautifully named 'bilberry bumblebee'! It just goes to show how much more wildlife you can attract and support when you don't use pesticides. All you have to do is plant some wild flowers and leave a corner of the grass to grow wild. Following these simple steps has helped me encourage wildlife to thrive in every corner of the garden!

June

There's never a dull moment in our 'glen' - there's always lots to tell! Plenty of battles being fought - over chicken food, chicken territories and gold finches.

So, let's start at the beginning...

Well, as I've mentioned in previous newsletters, we have a resident male pheasant called 'Cedric' who has been wandering around our place for several months. When he discovered the chicken food, our chickens (along with the neighbours' one), quickly made their feelings known: his presence would not be tolerated and he was chased out of the chicken run. But, because we live far from the main road, our chickens can basically go anywhere they please and when they are off wandering about, 'Cedric' creeps in and eats their chicken food. Sneaky! But, unfortunately, pheasants are not the smartest of animals and although he can get in, he doesn't have a clue how to get out of the chicken run - unless he's being chased by chickens! Several times I've had to tip-toe up to him and coax him out, but on a whole they are extremely stupid birds! Nice to look at, though!

Recently our neighbours got some new, normal sized chickens and some bantams (which are tiny and very cute). Unfortunately our chickens now think that our neighbours' garden is part of their territory and don't want the new chickens trespassing on it! I felt so sorry for one of the wee bantams when our hen 'Caramello' started to bully her, especially since she was minding her own business in her *own* garden! Our chickens respond really well to me, so I immediately called out to them and the wee bantam was spared.

And then there is the battle taking place over the gold finches...

Our neighbour, Mrs J, likes to feed 'her' gold finches. However, I like to feed the gold finches, too. So, Mrs J wasn't too happy when all the gold finches decided they liked the food I was serving in our garden better and didn't bother going back to dine in hers. But then again Mrs J has been hogging 'our' red squirrel, so fair's fair!

Also, we have spotted another bird species not previously seen in our garden; the bull finch. It was sitting on the fence eyeballing the gold finches tucking into the bird food and at first I didn't recognise the breed. My husband did though, confirming it was a bull finch. I've started writing down the different varieties of birds I've spotted in our garden and we now stand at 33 different species! I am so proud we have attracted so many different species of birds to our garden, especially when you think that when we moved here nine years ago there was nothing but grass, grass and more grass! Since then, we've planted lots of shrubs, trees and a wildlife hedge, and it has certainly paid off!

So, here are some tips to support wildlife in your garden:

If you have a small garden, planting some cornflowers and sunflowers will attract bees, bumblebees and butterflies and of course you can always put out some bird food, to attract, well you know... birds.

For medium sized gardens, why not plant some shrubs like berberis? They provide flowers, berries and shelter for all sorts of insects and birds. Or if you have enough space, why not plant a wildlife hedge consisting of hawthorn, rosehips and sloes (blackthorn)? A hedge provides shelter and slows down high winds too.

If you have a larger garden, try all of the above! Why not also plant trees like oak, ash or hazel? You might attract squirrels too! But make sure you plant large trees away from the house, because the roots will spread and you don't want them creeping under the foundation of your house!

But the best thing you can do for whatever size of garden you have is to ditch the chemicals! We need to live hand in hand with nature not work against it. Here endeth the lesson...

'Tell it to the Bees', the long awaited film I had made my 'extra' debut in (a couple of years ago!) was finally given a limited release to cinemas in July.

On a Sunday afternoon, my husband and I braved the rain to attend a screening at the MacRobert Centre in Stirling. No star-studded premiere; no red carpet; no paparazzi.

As the lights dimmed, excited and nervous I couldn't' help wonder whether I had made the final cut! And... I had... big time!

Now it's just a matter of waiting for the movie to be released on DVD!

July

I am writing this just one day after Stirling was flooded due to torrential rain. It was so bad that people had to be rescued by boat from the Stirling County rugby field! In Glendevon we had rain, but nothing on as big a scale as Stirling had - the whole of June's rainfall in the space of a few hours, or so I heard. Crazy, huh? But, d'you know something? I am so disappointed I wasn't in Stirling at the time of the thunderstorm, because I just simply love thunderstorms! My heart goes out to the businesses affected by water damage though, particularly those on Port Street! I hope the council finally realises that planting more trees and shrubs and keeping the drains empty are the way to prevent this from happening again and again. It's not the first time this has happened, either - a while back during another particularly heavy rainfall, I happened to look out of the shop's window in time to see a lady wading through ankle deep water, struggling to get into her car!

We had flooding once as well in Glendevon. The river Devon burst its banks and several cabins close to the river were flooded. If memory serves, that was back in the winter 2011 - the heavy snow we had melted because of a spell of heavy rain, so we were hit with a double whammy of water! That was years ago and lots of trees have been planted on the hills since then - and the river has never been as high as it was at that time. Thankfully our cottage has never been affected by water, it just runs past our house! We do need to be wary of high winds, though especially ones from the west. Since moving to Glendevon we've watched helplessly as several constructions (including a greenhouse!) were blown away by the strong winds! You live and learn but our chicken house has been built at the side of our house, safe and sheltered from the wind.

The vegetable garden seems to be slow this year and it's going to be a disastrous year for root vegetables. In my first lot of carrots only one germinated! I have sown them again, but I'm going to have to be patient to see if these will germinate and if they will even grow at all. The parsnips are the same: only a few came up and even the radishes haven't done much.

Something that is growing though, are the leafy vegetables! I don't think I've ever had this many salads and the white and red cabbages are on a roll too. I can even start harvesting kale, in the middle of summer which is unusual to say the least! Mind you, kale is not solely a winter vegetable, it grows all year round (like carrots) but because it is a hardy, leafy vegetable we tend to eat it mostly during winter time.

Unfortunately the runner beans and French beans are not doing much outside, either. Something's been chomping on the shoots; the weather's been too cold for them and now I've only got a couple of plants left.

Good job I can still go to the supermarket for my veggies!

My husband insisted I include 'Pepe' the pigeon in this month's blog, so here goes:

About a week ago, our cat found a racing pigeon sitting in the garden, struggling to get off the ground. Thankfully I noticed it too and rescued it before the cat could pounce. But because it was a ringed racing pigeon I kept it in a little box and fed it some grains (courtesy of the chickens) and water until it was fit enough to fly off again, which it did later that night. I really wanted to keep it, not for racing of course, but because it was such a darn cute little thing! However, I reported it to the 'lost racing pigeon' website (yes, there is such a thing!) and someone phoned me to tell me it originally came from Newcastle, but probably flew from either France or Brighton and got blown too far north! Poor thing....

August

I had a few well earned days off in July and rather than go to a busy camp site full of litter and noise, I just pitched my tent in my own back garden! My reasoning was this: "Why would I drive for hours to go to a camp site where cars are left idling; drunk people shouting and throwing up everywhere and children running around screaming, when I have a very isolated and quiet location right on my back doorstep?!" So that's where we set up camp - in our own back garden! Other benefits included: not having to share our toilet and shower with strangers (can't tell you how good that felt!); being able to cook in our own kitchen and (if we wanted) we could easily 'upgrade' and sleep in our own bed! I must say I did enjoy sleeping in the tent for a few nights - there is just nothing like sleeping outdoors, under the stars. And as an extra bonus the Glendevon road was closed (only open to residents) which meant that for a few weeks it was very quiet and peaceful in the garden.

On the first night we camped out I heard some scuffling outside the tent and was convinced it was a hedgehog, but getting out of your sleeping bag takes a lot longer than you might think, so when I finally emerged from the tent whatever it was had vanished.

The only signs that a hedgehog had visited our garden were the droppings it had left behind. Thanks for those.

On the second night we set up a 'night vision' camera in the hope we might be lucky enough to capture it on film. When I ventured out during the night, I once again heard something, shone my torch in the direction the sound came from, but couldn't see a thing. Nothing but darkness! The next morning there were more little droppings left behind - this time close to where the camera was set up, so I was convinced I had caught the little fella on camera. I was wrong. I couldn't believe it!! This little critter was proving to be very camera shy!

But I didn't give up, I set the camera up again and lo and behold, we finally managed to capture it on film over the next two nights! Proof positive we do have a hedgehog in the garden and I hadn't just imagined the whole thing. Except the droppings, they were very real.

The only down side to camping in your own back garden at this time of year is that you will have to pick the ripe fruit or it will rot. So, that's how my husband and I spent our 'holiday' - picking lots of red currants, black currants and masses of strawberries, cleaning them, then freezing them until I have some free time and use them to make jam.

So, harvest wise, we have been eating (well, more like stuffing our faces with) punnet after punnet of deliciously sweet home grown strawberries. And do you know what? I'm nowhere near sick of the sight of them... yet. That could be because I know I can't eat them for the rest of the year. Mind you, after having harvested a whopping 20 kg (44 lbs) of strawberries it won't be too long before I start getting tired of eating them!

It's been a bit of a mixed year with vegetables to be honest; all leafy vegetables seem to be doing really well; the cabbages are growing fast; the chard is also growing well and the foliage of the potato plants is the highest I've ever seen it.

But other things have just been a downright disaster this year! There's no other word for it. Well, 'catastrophe' will also do. Of the fifteen runner bean plants I planted; only four are now beginning to slowly crawl up the canes staked into the ground. The rest have been eaten by slugs and what the slugs haven't finished, the pigeons have polished off. I have sowed some late French beans in their place, but it needs to stay warm if they are to produce anything at all.

My sweet pepper plants are also a disaster this year; they were doing really well, some even producing peppers, until red spider mite took hold and destroyed them.

I have asked an allotment group on Facebook for some advice and they suggested chilli and garlic spray, which I have now been using, so only time will tell if my poor plants will recover or not. The problem is that a greenhouse is an enclosed, unnatural environment. The air is more or less stagnant, there is no natural water and natural predators can't find the plants. But it isn't all bad news, though. My tomatoes are looking especially plump!

Sigh....! Who ever said organic gardening was easy?

September

It's now time to start harvesting the fruits of my labour in the garden and as always there have been some winners and losers this year. Let's start with the winners: as I mentioned last month, the leafy vegetables are growing incredibly well. We will soon be making our sauerkraut again and all I will eat this week is coleslaw, colcannon (a traditional dish made from potatoes and cabbage) and fried rice with cabbage - that's a lot of cabbage I hear you say! You see, one of the big cabbages has split and I need to use it up! Sometimes cabbages grow too fast and too big and the head just, well, splits, or... maybe an axe wielding maniac with a cabbage fixation has been rampaging through my garden! I have also harvested at least two kilograms of chard (from just a few plants) and there is more to come. There is also lots of kale to freeze and enjoy later during the colder months ahead. The winter cabbages are looking healthy too and growing as we speak... er, as I type.

Unfortunately there are plenty of losers in the garden this year too. I have only managed to grow two courgettes from three plants! Sadly, there will be no turnips (neeps) this year, but thankfully my second sowing of swedes paid off and we can enjoy some of these instead, but it just won't be the same. This has really got me baffled, because our neighbours (and one of the shop reps who also grows her own veggies) have had no success with turnips this year either, despite it being such a common Scottish vegetable and one which normally performs well whatever the weather throws at it. Carrots have not grown either (nor for anyone else I've spoken to) but the onions have grown pretty well. I just hope these will store well too; it is always a challenge to dry them out when the weather is so changeable.

Remember the poor sweet pepper plants I mentioned last time? Well, I followed some advice I was given by the Facebook group and lo-and-behold the plants have survived and the peppers are even beginning to turn red now! They are not that big, but at least we'll have some sweet peppers this year! The runner beans are finally flowering but it might be a case of 'too little too late', but you never know. If we get a warm September I might still get some runner beans. The French beans in both the greenhouse and the garden have produced more than last year, so that was a pleasant surprise. I grew a purple variety this time round which were easy to pick, mainly because it was so easy to spot them! They lose their colour when you cook them, but they still looked pretty on the plant.

What are we going to do with our consistently broody hen 'Punky'? When a hen is broody, she won't lay any eggs and just sits on an empty nest all day long. If you remember 'Punky' is the stupid one, sorry, but it's true. She was last broody a few months ago and now she just sits there waiting for non-existent eggs to hatch... again. The other two hens ('Tufty' and 'Caramello') are hardly ever broody and just enjoy life - foraging in the fields surrounding our house. Despite the fact that 'Punky' has hardly laid any eggs, I still have to admit that she is my favourite... just don't tell the other two! Before she became broody, the chickens had to stay in their run for a few days and while the other two hens were going 'stir crazy', trashing the place, 'Punky' simply stood in the corner looking up at me as if to say: "It wasn't me, I didn't do anything, mummy. It was those two - I'm a good girl!"

Who would have thought I would become so attached to my feathery little friends? Not me. Not in a million years!

October

I am writing this on 'Global Climate Strike day' - did any of our readers get involved, too? This day was all about reducing CO_2 in the atmosphere and to confront the growing climate crisis we face and to help secure a better future for all of us...

So, here are some things we can do ourselves to limit our CO_2 emissions:

Drive less and/or fly less: have a 'staycation'. Britain has got some really lovely places to visit too!

Buy less: before buying something new, consider whether the old one is really broken and/or if it really needs replaced 'new'. Also; 'best before' dates on food products usually means they are still okay to consume, 'use by dates' are not.

Grow some or most of your own vegetables and fruit: this way you get a free 'work out' and you are reducing mileage used to transport vegetables to your home.

Or if you haven't got a garden: only eat British grown fruit and veg; again less transport involved and a more varied diet throughout the year.

Plant a native tree in your garden: for a large garden, choose oak, ash or rowan. Or for a small garden choose alder, bird cherry or holly. And enjoy the many species of birds that will pay you a 'flying' visit!

Eat less meat, no meat or only 'wild' meat: It takes many kilograms of grain to feed every 1 kg of cow and these guys are big! These grains could be used to feed us too. Besides this, a cow emits CO_2 and methane (from you know what and where), whereas plants absorb CO_2.

As you know I have been growing my own vegetables and fruit for quite some time now. Some years ago a small plant grew beneath our bird feeder from oats and wheat that had spilled out of it and fallen onto the ground (those birds are such messy eaters!). I collected the grains from that plant and re-sowed them. I did that for some years and now I can sow my own little bed of oats and wheat. The birds are happy too, of course, but now the birds have expanded their 'home-grown' seeds and sowed (dropped) rapeseeds from the bird feeder. I've let the plants grow again and they are now huge! I collected the rapeseeds in September and managed to fill a jar full to the brim (and still had some left over)! Busy bees these birds! Or busy birds these birds to be more exact!

The birds aren't the only creatures that have been busy this month. So have the spiders in our greenhouse! It's no secret I'm not too keen on spiders (bit of an understatement there!) and the greenhouse at this time of year is a hotspot for the larger sized 'eight legged freaks'. I asked my husband to kindly ask them to leave while I waited outside, whimpering. We are now the not-so-proud owners of 'Roxy' the spider, 'Harriet' the spider, 'Shelob' the spider and 'Rana the spider. We named them after our neighbours' dogs, in order of size, from smallest to largest. Well, except Shelob who is named after the giant spider from 'Lord of the Rings').

Poor old Punky! Our neighbours' new chickens seem to have completely taken over the place and banished our lot far from the house. At long last Punky has stopped feeling broody, but when she came off her nest, she was missing her 2 pals, Caramello and Tufty, who were hiding from our neighbours' bullying hens. Now she's too scared to come out of the run. I think she has been picked on one too many times by the neighbours' chickens and doesn't quite know what to do about it. Some days she even goes to bed by 3 o'clock in the afternoon! I feel sorry for her because she is all alone in the run, on the plus side it does mean she has access to all the food available and gets extra titbits too, so every cloud and all that. I guess 'Punky the Punkster' is the new star of the newsletter, albeit a completely different one from 'The Hooligan' aka the most famous chicken in Stirling. Remember her?

> **Did you know...**
>
> ... although there are only three houses in our tiny glen, this is the **second book** to be published on the subject of living here?

One thing I'm going to try not to do next year is complain about my vegetables not growing before the end of October, because despite the very slow start, everything is now catching up... big time! I honestly thought I wasn't going to get any cucumbers this year, but the 4 plants are now producing lots of fruit and I've been busy pickling them. Also the runner beans I wrote about some months ago are finally growing, nothing like the 6 kg we had last year, but we'll probably end up with enough for a couple of meals! And the courgettes... they are massive! Sadly, we also had potato blight in one of our potato crops, this is the first time this has ever happened and we are gutted! We are so remote, we are generally safe from blight, but apparently this year it managed to track us down! So, I have boiled, mashed and frozen the tatties which were affected and JP, my hubby, boiled, cut chips and froze them.

The growing season will all end soon and by the time this newsletter goes out I'll probably have harvested the last of the courgettes and runner beans. Never mind though, because I still have some carrots and parsnips in the ground, waiting to be picked!

As long as I have something to do in the garden I have a purpose. I am happy and content.

Although 'The Hooligan' is no longer with us, and the growing conditions in Glendevon can often be bad, I can honestly say - hand on heart - that life here is good.

And after all, who can ask for anything more?

Mighty Oaks from Little Acorns Grow

I have a dream... of leaving this world a greener place.

I'm trying to leave more trees when I die than there were when I first came into this world, knowing that my legacy to this world will hopefully be some tall, magnificent oak trees and lots of other types of native trees. As a matter of fact, I want to leave a small forest behind and create an environment which is beneficial to wildlife and humans alike.

In Autumn of last year I sowed (or should I say planted?) acorns and seeds from other trees in big pots next to my house. I waited. And waited. And waited. I was on the verge of giving up, because by the beginning of May there was still no sign of any of the seeds germinating.

It's all about patience.

I can be impatient sometimes, especially when growing things. But lo and behold, after my patience was tested all spring, my acorns finally germinated in mid May!

And, yes, I know it usually takes over 60 years for an oak tree to grow to a decent size, but just seeing it grow into a tree would be good enough for me, just in case I'm not around that long.

I just have to keep reminding myself to be patient!

Isn't it incredible that from these tiny plants, giant, majestic oak trees grow?

I've started to call them 'my oak babies'.

We also have an 'oak toddler' in the garden too, which is a tree we bought over 4 years ago when it was already a year old. It's grown taller than me already, but still looks very small compared to the oak trees in the surrounding countryside.

It was just acorns that germinated this time, but I'm going to sow other trees this Autumn again and make sure the soil conditions are right for each specific species of tree. Maybe I'll dig up some soil from underneath the appropriate tree and sow the corresponding seeds in that.

Who knows? Maybe one day, I'll have grown an entire forest of trees!

And at the end of my life I can rest peacefully knowing I've generated more trees than I've used during my lifetime. My final wish would then be to be buried beneath a tree, preferably one I grew myself! But that would all depend on how long I've got left...

One thing is for sure, though. The 'oak babies' are likely to live on long after I am nothing but a distant memory.

And one day they will become 'oak mothers' themselves!

'The Beechgrove Garden' Affair

Sometime in late 2014, I wrote a letter to the production team behind one of my favourite TV shows, **'The Beechgrove Garden'**. My husband and I needed their help. We felt we could benefit from their knowledge and horticultural expertise...

Dear Madam/Sir,

After watching last night's episode of Beechgrove Garden (Thursday 12th June) - the one in which Carole pays a visit to Old Allangrange House garden on the Black Isle - I was inspired to write to you.

Ever since my husband and I bought our house 3 years ago, we've been working on transforming our garden into a wildlife friendly garden, too. This has been a long term project and, like Jay Jay we've also enlisted the help of a number of wwoofers to give us a hand over the last couple of years.

Like Jay Jay's garden, our (front) garden was also essentially just a field, which we have now transformed into a mixed wild flower border. The main differences between both gardens is that ours is a lot smaller and sits at 270m (885ft) above sea level, which means it's a little bit colder and everything takes a little bit longer to bloom.

Our objective this year is to create a 'five senses garden' in the back, complete with a pond and boggy area. This garden will consist of 5 borders with a variety of plants to appeal to each of our 5 senses: smell, sight, hearing, touch and taste and also a bed of medicinal plants for use at home. As the owner of my own health food shop I have an understanding of each herb and their individual health benefits.

Of course we also grow our own vegetables organically and although the garden is only ¼ acre, we are more or less able to be self-sufficient in vegetables and fruit (from which we also make our own wine and preserves).

Ultimately, we hope to open our garden to the public in time for the Scotland's Garden Scheme in a few years time.

If you are interested, my husband and I would like to invite you to film our garden as it is now and/or at some point in the future when the garden is in full bloom.

I have attached a few pictures showing the front garden as it was and how it looks now and the back garden as it was/is.

Kind regards,

Josine Atsma
Glendevon

Although I featured some of our experience filming **'The Beechgrove Garden'** in the May 2015 issue of our newsletter, there simply wasn't enough room to tell the full story.

So, what follows is the full, unedited version!

That's another experience we've got under our belt!!

Last Thursday, BBC2's 'The Beechgrove Garden' came to our place in Glendevon, Central Scotland to show us how to create a bog garden.

We had a fantastic day! The weather was dry although a bit windy (in true Glendevon-style). JP and I even got sunburned! The film crew were a very friendly bunch and we had lots of fun.

Firstly, George Anderson and the film crew went to film his introduction to camera. I have no idea what was said, though, because they went filming on the path leading up to our house while we stayed back at the house. Unfortunately, my lip reading skills are not that good!

I guess we'll just have to wait until it's on TV.

Next, George, JP and I had to explain what the plan for the day was.

JP and I are creating a 'five senses' garden and the bog area is to separate the 'vision' section from the 'smell' borders. So, I was filmed talking to George, reminding him about the five senses; smell, taste, touch, vision and hearing. However, as I was being filmed for the first time in my life, my nerves got the better of me and I kept forgetting what the fifth sense was! In the end we had to do it again and again. Sometimes I would mention 'scent' and 'smell' which of course are the same thing! And then there was the issue of filming with only one camera, which meant we had to do everything at least three times from different angles.

Once all the introductions were 'in the can' we all started digging over the bog area. Our two wwoofers staying with us were a great help and enjoyed being in front of the camera too.

Meanwhile, JP started building a wee wooden bridge in the background.

Because everything had to be done three or four times, I ended up digging the same bit of ground over and over. Raking the whole thing over was no different.

Camera man: "Could you rake that again?" Me: "Absolutely, nothing better to do - I've only done it four times so far!"

Again planting and moving plants was the same - multiple takes, from different angles. Firstly we had to carry the trays with the plants to the bog area at least three times.

Then the cameraman would suddenly say: "Stop!" And we all froze in whatever what position we happened to be in, until he had changed camera angle, then he would shout: "Okay, and walk!" So we began moving again as if nothing had happened.

Who knew that for a meagre five or six minutes of screen time you need to film for an entire day?

Presenter George Anderson and 'The Beechgrove Garden' film crew (together with our two wwoofers) arrived on our doorstep at 9am to help us. And by 4.30pm all the excitement was over. It seems like ages ago now!

I wasn't all that nervous about the whole thing to be honest, maybe the odd butterfly or two. I'm more apprehensive about it being shown on TV!

I certainly didn't expect to get a microphone pinned to me and a transmitter stuffed into my back pocket the moment they arrived! I suppose it made sense, how else would they be able to record what we were saying?

The chickens weren't the least bit camera shy and behaved very professionally - particularly 'The Hooligan'. Can't believe I'm saying that. I bet you're as astonished as I was! Arriving 'on set' promptly, the chickens spotted us digging and came over to us in force to help us 'find worms' (so they could eat them, naturally). 'The Hooligan' is a bit of a diva, I reckon. I think she thought the camera was there solely for her benefit.

"I'm ready for my close up now, Ms Director!"

Upstaged by a chicken. It's all about her...
but, when isn't it? She's always got to be the
'star' of the show!

F@*#!

A Conversation with 'The Hooligan'

Not so long ago, in a garden not too far away... 'the Chick-Peas' came up to me to complain about the behaviour of the ill tempered 'The Hooligan'.

The conversation went something like this:

Me: "Hello Chick-Peas, how was your day?"

Chick-Peas: "It was horrible! 'The Hooligan' was blocking the exit to the garden and pecking and swearing at us! We really don't like that one!"

Me: "Okay, I'll have a word with her."

I turn to 'The Hooligan'.

Me: "Hello, Hooli Bully. I've had some complaints from the Chick-Peas about you bullying them. What do you have to say for yourself?"

The Hooligan: "First of all, don't call me Hooli Bully! I hate that! Just call me 'The Hooligan'! Secondly, those new chickens are a bunch of *#**@#!!"

Me: "Whoa... calm down! Alright? Just tell me why you don't like them and what you did."

The Hooligan: "Those little *@#*#!!! have no idea who the boss is around here. I want to go to bed first. I want to eat first. I want to get out of the run first. And I want to be in the garden first!! Yet, they refuse to listen to me. They run out before I can get out of bed, they start eating without my permission and now they want to eat the first worms in the garden too! I can't let that happen! So, all I did was block the exit and told them to f... f... cluck off!!'"

Me: "Right, okay. Maybe you shouldn't use so much effing and blinding. Maybe you should..."

The Hooligan: "Right that's it, I'm off. I'm sick of listening to you! I'll do and say what and when I like. You can't stop me!!!

And off she runs.

Me: "Sigh... there really is no reasoning with that chicken. I'll go to the Chick-Peas and tell them what happened."

Chick-Peas: "Oh no, there is 'The Hooligan' again! She's storming towards us! She's coming to beat us up for squealing on her. Let's hide!! Aaarrrggh!"

The Hooligan: "Wait 'til I get my wings on you, you little b#*@#s?! I'll get you for this!!"

Me: "Oh dear, 'The Hooligan' is chasing the Chick-Peas. I'll lure her away with some bird food. That usually works."

Me: "Chicky, chicky! Come chicky, chicky!"

'The Hooligan' stops in her tracks and runs to the bird food, leaving the Chick-Peas bewildered, but safe. For now.

Peace has been restored to our garden. All is well again in Glendevon, until the next time...

Tips on Living Life with Less Plastic

It's all over the news, **plastic is everywhere**! From the remotest parts of Mongolia to the deepest oceans! Here are some tips on how to reduce the amount of plastic you use.

By starting with a few small changes you can make all the difference. Firstly, don't throw away all plastic items you have in the home. The first step is to keep using plastic tubs, plastic seeding trays, plastic toys etc. You don't have to buy everything again brand new!

All food grade plastic is suitable for reusing over and over again, but single-use plastic, like plastic water bottles, is not!!

The second step is to become more aware of when and where you are more likely to use plastic. Do you buy coffee on the way to work? Why not invest in a reusable cup? Or make coffee at home or at your workplace - you'll save around a whopping £600 a year if you stop buying on-the-go coffee! Are you planning to go shopping? Don't forget to bring your own carrier bag. Are you going to buy olives or other foods from a deli counter or buy a takeaway soup? Simply bring your own tub and have that filled instead. Don't be embarrassed to ask - a lot of people are doing it!

Then there is the issue of food wrapped in plastic. There are several things you can do: sign up to a vegetable box scheme (organic, naturally), grow your own food where possible, or just take loose fruit and vegetables to the supermarket checkout (bananas are already wrapped in their own skin!) or seek out a local milk supplier who uses glass bottles.

A lot of plastics are used in the home too and thankfully there are lots of alternatives available. Most independent health food stores refill washing-up liquid and laundry liquid bottles from companies such as Bio D and Ecover. Various other household cleaning products are available in 5 litre sizes from the same independent health food shops. Sometimes you need to ask them to order these in and most will be happy to do so.

Don't use clingfilm, apparently you can easily make it yourself using beeswax (or soy wax) and cotton cloth (beeswax blocks can also be found in specialist farm shops and health food shops)

Ditch the plastic dish brush and use a loofah sponge instead. These are made from natural plant material and when they are worn out, you simply chuck them on top of the compost heap or pop them in the food recycling bin.

Sauerkraut Recipe

Because sauerkraut is made using a process called **lacto-fermentation**, it contains healthy bacteria which not only preserves the sauerkraut but is also beneficial for your own internal health. It's naturally cholesterol free, fat free and high in vitamin C.

Ingredients:

3 kg white cabbage

10 g peppercorns

20 g juniper berries

30 g salt

Preparation

Making sauerkraut is super easy! All you need to find is a proper sauerkraut crock (which is available to buy online).

Then all you do is wash a white cabbage, shred it as thinly as you can (a food processor is ideal, but you can also do it by hand), layer the sliced cabbage with a little bit of salt and juniper berries or caraway seeds in the crock. Pound it with your fists (very therapeutic!) or something heavy (and clean) until there is a layer of water covering the cabbage. Leave it in a warm place to ferment for around 2 months. Then move it to a cooler environment.

After about 2-3 months the sauerkraut should be ready to eat. Don't worry if there is a layer of white mould floating on top, this is not harmful and can just be removed to reveal the delicious ready-to-eat sauerkraut underneath. It is likely that the smell coming off the white mould on top is foul smelling too, but this is totally normal! The sauerkraut itself should smell normal.

Sauerkraut stores for a long time - as long as it is kept in a cool place. I'm still eating mine in February or March!

Sauerkraut crocks are not easily available in the UK I believe, but all it does is keep the air out, while letting the fermenting fumes escape at the same time. So, if you can find a way of doing this, perhaps via an airlock used for making wine, you can create your own fermenting vessel.

Atjar Tjampoer Recipe

This is a sweet and sour pickled side dish you would bring to any Indonesian table serving rice, but I have it with my own **nasi goreng** (another Dutch/Indonesian dish).

Ingredients:

350 g carrots
250 g white cabbage
100 g sweet red pepper
1 or 2 onions
100 g bean sprouts
10 g fresh ginger root
$1/2$ chilli pepper
8 peppercorns
1 tsp turmeric
Salt
3 tbsp light muscovado sugar
1 tbsp oil
2 dl cider vinegar

Preparation

Shred all the vegetables (apart from the bean sprouts) or cut them into really small strips.

Boil the vegetables in a big pan for about one minute, put them in a colander and rinse/cool under cold running water. Add the bean sprouts and mix well.

Put the vegetable mix into sterilised jars.

Using a pestle and mortar; mix the ginger, chilli pepper, peppercorns, sugar, turmeric and salt into a thick paste.

Heat the oil in a frying pan and quickly fry the spice paste for around 2 minutes until you can smell the spices. Add the cider vinegar and heat gently.

When the spice/vinegar mix has reached boiling point, add to the jars and fill completely. Press down the vegetables until the vinegar is higher than the vegetables.

Screw the lid on immediately and leave to cool. After a while you will hear a 'plop'. That means the jars are now vacuum sealed and can be stored for up to half a year (although sometimes I keep them for over a year). You can also check by pressing down the 'dome' in the lid. If you can't press it, it's vacuum sealed.

How to sterilise jars

Wash in hot soapy water and rinse thoroughly. Put them upside down in a hot oven (120°C) and leave until they are dry. The temperature in the oven kills all the bacteria.